DEATH IN THE CITY

FRANCIS A. SCHAEFFER

DEATH IN THE CITY

INTER-VARSITY PRESS

INTER-VARSITY PRESS

Inter-Varsity Fellowship
39 Bedford Square, London WC1

© FRANCIS A. SCHAEFFER

First published in the USA by Inter-Varsity Press, Chicago

First British Edition August 1969

STANDARD BOOK NUMBER 85110 347 2

Printed in Great Britain by Hazell Watson & Viney Ltd,
Aylesbury, Bucks

CONTENTS

PREFACE

This book is based upon a series of lectures given at Wheaton College, Illinois, 30 September–4 October 1968. I have not attempted to remove all the marks of the lecture form.

It is imperative in our generation to bring historic Christianity into contact with twentieth-century man and his intellectual and cultural questions. This was the theme of my two earlier books *Escape From Reason* and *The God Who Is There*. But these answers must be firmly related to exposition of Scripture and it is this which the present volume seeks to do. In addition we must demonstrate that the Personal-Infinite God exists, an aspect covered by my wife in her book *L'Abri*. All these elements must be kept together as a unity. To separate them would grieve the Holy Spirit and sever the link with modern man.

May God grant us reformation, revival and constructive revolution in the orthodox, evangelical church.

FRANCIS A. SCHAEFFER

We live in a post-Christian world. What should be our perspective as individuals, as orthodox Christians, as those who would claim to be Bible-believing? How should we look at this post-Christian world and function as Christians in it?

This book will try to answer these questions. I will begin by asserting a proposition concerning the basic need of the orthodox church in our post-Christian world. Then I will consider that proposition in the biblical context of the books of Romans, Lamentations and Jeremiah. Throughout we shall look at the situation we face in the modern world and the perspective we must have as Christians in that world.

The proposition is concerning reformation and revival. This is the basic need of the orthodox, evangelical church in our moment of history.

The church in our generation needs reformation, revival and constructive revolution.

At times men think of the two words 'reformation' and 'revival' as standing in contrast one to the other. But this is a mistake. Both words are related to the word 'restore'.

Reformation refers to a restoration to pure doctrine; revival refers to a restoration in the Christian's life. Reformation speaks of a return to the teachings of Scripture; revival speaks of a life brought into its proper relationship to the Holy Spirit.

The great moments of church history have come when these two restorations have simultaneously come into action, so that the church has returned to pure doctrine and the lives of the Christians in the church have known the power of the Holy Spirit. There cannot be true revival unless there has been reformation; and reformation is not complete without revival.

Such a combination of reformation and revival would be revolutionary in our day—revolutionary in our individual lives as Christians, revolutionary not only in reference to the liberal church but constructively revolutionary in the evangelical, orthodox church as well.

We need to be those who know the reality of both reformation and revival, so that this poor dark world may have an exhibition of a portion of the church returned to both pure doctrine and Spirit-filled life.

The latter portion of the first chapter of Romans speaks of man as he is, and two verses tell how he came to be in that position. Romans 1:21, 22 states, 'Because that, when they knew God, they glorified him not as God, neither gave thanks; but became vain in their reasoning.' It is important that we follow the Greek here with the word 'reasoning' and not 'imagination' (as the Authorized Version renders it), because the emphasis is not on what our generation uses the word 'imagination' to express, but on what it calls 'reasoning'. What is involved here is in men's thinking, in that which is cognitive, in thought processes, in comprehension. Thus, they 'became vain in their reasoning, and their foolish heart was darkened. Professing themselves to be wise, they became fools.' When the Scripture speaks of man being thus foolish, it does not mean he is only religiously foolish. Rather, it means that he has accepted a position that is intellectually foolish not only in regard to what the Bible says but also in regard to what exists, the universe and its form, and the 'mannishness' of man. In turning away from God and the truth which He has given, man has thus become *foolishly* foolish in regard to what man is and what the universe is. He is left with a position in which he cannot live, and he is caught in a multitude of intellectual and personal tensions.

Such is the biblical position regarding man. And if we are going to begin to think of reformation and revival, we must have the same mentality God has concerning the position of man.

The Scripture tells us how man came into that situation: 'Because that, when they knew God, they glorified him not as God, neither gave thanks'; therefore, they became foolish in their reasoning, in their comprehension, in their lives. This passage relates to the original fall, but it does not speak only about the original fall. It speaks of any period where men knew the truth and deliberately turned away from it.

Many periods of history could be spoken of in this way. From the biblical viewpoint there was a time when the ancestors of the people of India knew the truth and turned away, a time when the ancestors of the people of Africa knew the truth and turned away. This is true of people anywhere who now do not know the truth. But if we are looking across the history of the world to see those times when men knew the truth and turned away, let us say emphatically that this is exhibited nowhere in history so clearly in such a short expanse of years as in our own generation. We who live in the northern European culture, including America and Canada, have seen this verse in our generation carried out with desperate strength. Men of our time knew the truth and yet turned away, turned away not only from the biblical truth, the religious truth of the Reformation, but turned away from the total culture built upon that truth, including the balance of freedom and form which the Reformation brought forth in northern Europe in the state and in society, a balance which has never been known anywhere in the world before.

Having turned away from the knowledge given by God, man has now lost the whole Christian culture. In Europe, including Britain, it took many years; in the United States only a few decades. In the United States in the short span from the twenties to the sixties we have seen a complete shift. Of course not everyone in the United States in the twenties was a Christian, but in general there was a Christian consensus. Now that consensus is completely gone. Ours is a post-Christian world in which Christianity, not only in the number of Christians but in cultural emphasis and cultural result, is now in the absolute minority. To ask young people to maintain the status quo is folly. The status quo is no longer ours. In the last four decades the change has come in *every portion* and in *every part* of life. If in the twenties you had distributed a questionnaire in a place like Columbus Circle in New York, you would have found that most of the people may not personally have been Christians, but they at least would have had an idea of what Christianity was. Trafalgar Square about 1890 would have been the same. But if today you distributed a questionnaire in these places, you would find that almost every man you asked would have little or no concept of true Christianity. When we begin to think of them and preach the gospel to them, we must begin with the fact that they have no knowledge of biblical Christianity. But it is more than this, for the whole culture has shifted from Christian to post-Christian.

We cannot take this lightly. It is a horrible thing for a man like myself to look back and see my country and my culture go down the drain in my own lifetime. It is a horrible thing that forty years ago you could move across the United States and almost everyone, even non-Christians, would have known what the gospel was. A horrible thing that thirty to forty years ago our culture was built on the Christian consensus and now we are in an absolute minority.

As Christians in this period of history we are faced with some crucial questions, the first one being this: What is to be our perspective as we acknowledge the post-Christian character of our culture?

Referring to Romans 1:21, 22 again we read: 'Because that, when they knew God, they glorified him not as God, neither gave thanks; but became vain in their reasoning, and their foolish heart was darkened. Professing themselves to be wise, they became fools.' Verse 18 tells us the result of man's turning away from and rebelling against the truth he knows: 'For the wrath of God is revealed from heaven against all ungodliness and unrighteousness of men, who hold the truth in unrighteousness.' Man is justly under the wrath of the God who really exists and who deals with men on the basis of His character, and if the justice of that wrath is obvious concerning any generation, it is our own.

There is only one perspective we can have of the post-Christian world of our generation: an understanding that our culture and our country is under the wrath of God. *Our* country is under the wrath of God. Northern European culture is under the wrath of God. It will not do to say how great we are. It will not do to cover up the difference between the consensus today and the consensus of a Christian world. The last few generations have trampled upon the truths of the Reformation and all that those truths have brought forth. And we are under the wrath of God. This is the perspective we must have if we are going to understand what reformation, revival and a true constructive revolution will mean.

What, then, should be our message in such a world—to the world, to the church, and to ourselves?

We do not have to guess what God would say about this because there was a period of history, biblical history, which greatly parallels our day. That is the day of Jeremiah. The book of Jeremiah and the book of Lamentations show how God looks at a culture which knew Him and deliberately turned away. But this is not just the character of Jeremiah's day of apostasy. It is my day. It is your day. And if we are going to help our own generation, our perspective must be that of Jeremiah, that weeping prophet Rembrandt so magnificently pictured weeping over Jerusalem, yet in the midst of his tears speaking without mitigating his message of judgment to a people who had had so much yet turned away.

In Jeremiah 1:2, 3, we are given the historic setting in which Jeremiah spoke. 'To whom the word of the Lord came in the days of Josiah the son of Amon king of Judah, in the thirteenth year of his reign. It came also in the days of Jehoiakim the son of Josiah king of Judah, unto the end of the eleventh year of Zedekiah the son of Josiah king of Judah, unto the carrying away of Jerusalem captive in the fifth month.' Here is Jeremiah rooted in history, during the reign of the last five kings before the nation was carried into the Babylonian captivity.

The Bible puts its religious teaching in a historical setting. It is quite the opposite of the new theology and existential thought, quite the opposite of the twentieth century's reduction of religion to subjective projection. Scripture relates true religion to space-time history which may be expressed in normal literary form. And that is important, because our generation takes the word 'religion' and turns it into something which is no more than psychological or sociological.

The Bible also has another emphasis. Not all that occurs in space-time history is explainable on the basis of natural cause and effect, for example, economic, military and psychological forces. Most modern men explain all of history this way, but the Bible does not. The Bible says that there is a true significant space-time history which God has made. Of course, history must be understood to be partially a product of the economic forces, of the flow of cultural thought, of military power, and so forth. If we were to study Jeremiah in detail, we would see various forces present: the great countries, Egypt on one side, Babylon on the other— tremendous external and internal forces. But history is not to be explained only on this basis. For a holy and a loving God really exists, and He works into the significant history which exists. He works in history on the basis of His character, and when His people and their culture turn away from Him, He works in history in judgment.

We must understand that the 'Christian culture' of Jeremiah's day was disintegrating into a 'post-Christian culture'. The holy God was dealing with that culture according to His character. Historical results were not just a product of chance, nor merely of mechanical, economic and psychological forces. It was God working into that history as His people turned away from Him.

In Lamentations 1:1 Jeremiah speaks of the city of Jerusalem: 'How doth the city sit solitary, that was full of people!' Jerusalem, a city which used to be close to God, has been changed by the choice of significant men. They have turned away from Him when they knew Him, and now their city is under siege. There is death in the city.

Furthermore, in Lamentations 1:9, Jeremiah says with brilliant realism: 'Her filthiness is in her skirts.' God's betrothed—this people and their total culture—has become filthy in her skirts. She is filled with spiritual adultery, and God says, 'Her filthiness is in her skirts; she remembereth not her last end.' This last phrase is tremendous: she does not remember her last, her final, end.

Two factors are involved. She has forgotten what her end will be if she turns from God, but, even more fundamental, she has forgotten her purpose as a nation—she has forgotten her relationship to God. She has forgotten what was recorded in the Pentateuch, that the chief end is to love God. She has forgotten her purpose as the people of God. She has even forgotten the purpose of man. For man is not just a chance configuration of atoms in the slip-stream of meaningless, chance history. No. Man, made in the image of God, has a purpose—to be in relationship to the God who is there. And whether it is in Jeremiah's day, or in our own last three generations, the effect is the same. Man forgets his purpose and thus he forgets who he is and what life means.

It was my generation and the generation that preceded me that forgot. The younger generation is not primarily to be blamed. Those who are struggling today, those who are far away and doing that which is completely contrary to the Christian conscience, are not first to be blamed. It is my generation and the generation that preceded me who turned away. Today we are left not only with a religion and a church without meaning, but we are left with a culture without meaning. Man *himself* is dead.

Jeremiah says this of God's people who turned away in his day: 'Her filthiness is in her skirts; she remembereth not her last end; therefore she came down wonderfully: she had no comforter.' Because the Jewish nation did not remember the purpose of its existence, it came down wonderfully. The people could not find a comforter.

What marks our own generation? It is the fact that modern man thinks there is nobody home in the universe. *Nobody* to love man, nobody to comfort him, even while he seeks desperately to find comfort in the limited, finite, horizontal relationships of life. But it does not work—in his art, in his music, or anywhere else. In his literature, in his drama, it does not work. In the sexual act, in human relationships, he finds only the devastatingly sterile and the dreadfully ugly.

The Jews had tried Egypt; they had tried Babylon, but there was no comfort, for the true Comforter was gone. In pornography, hedonism, and much else our generation has tried a thousand Egypts and a thousand Babylons. But men have come down wonderfully because they have forgotten who man is and what his final purpose is. The true Comforter is gone.

But in Lamentations 1:11, Jeremiah continues: 'All her people sigh, they seek bread; they have given their pleasant things for meat to relieve the soul.' 'To relieve the soul' may be translated 'to make the soul come again'. In a city under

17

siege, these Jews were physically starving; they were giving everything for bread.

Today most men in the West are not physically starving. In fact many in America and Europe are suffocating in the stench of a completely affluent society. But, no matter what their philosophic and intellectual system is, men, being made in the image of God, have human hungers that need to be satisfied. To some the major need is intellectual; they must have answers. So they look into existential philosophy and linguistic analysis. But there is no final answer there. Other people have a deep longing for beauty. So they try to produce beauty out of their own fallenness and self-expression of fallenness. But the final answer and true comfort are not there.

A hunger for beauty. A hunger for answers. Still other men are hungry for moral realities. Many modern sociologists, for example, are troubled by the lack of a firm basis for moral and social form. How is man to find firm categories to distinguish social good from social evil? They try relativism, the concept of social contract, and various types of totalitarianism, and comfort slips through their fingers.

And many men are hungry for love, for God has made man to love. So our generation has turned to sex as a fulfilment of the need for love in the human heart. But it does not work. I have known couples who have talked half through the night and for many nights. What for? Because, being consistent in their non-Christian world, they were seeking some kind of human relationship in trying to find just one sentence that they could say and could exhaust together to begin to have meaningful human contact. But being finite they failed. So man cries out, 'I am starving.'

The hand of God is down into our culture in judgment

and men are hungry. Unlike Zeus whom men imagined hurling down great thunderbolts, God has turned away in judgment as our generation turned away from Him and He is allowing cause and effect to take its course in history.

God can bring His judgment in one of two ways: either by direct intervention in history or by the turning of the wheels of history. Often it is the peripheral blessings that flow from the gospel, when freed from the Christian base, which then become the things of judgment in the next generation. One may consider, for example, freedom. It is the results of the Reformation in the northern European world which gave us a balance of form and freedom in the area of the state and society: freedom for women, freedom for children, freedom in the area of the state under law. And yet, when once we are away from the Christian base, it is this very freedom, now as freedom without form, that is bringing a judgment upon us in the turning wheels of history.

As the wheels of history turn, our generation feels, as Proust said, the 'dust of death' upon everything. And as he feels the transitoriness of the present life, he tries either to elongate it or, through all kinds of strange and devious devices, to give hope for life after death. Thus we find a strange thing: men who are naturalists and yet seek seances with those who have died. In men like Ingmar Bergman we find a denial of the existence of God but a growing interest in demonology.

As the Jews of Jeremiah's day were hungry for bread and had no comforter, our post-Christian world is hungry in state and society and in the individual longings of the heart, for it too has turned in our own day from the only sufficient Comforter.

Therefore, if we are going to understand anything about

reformation, revival and real constructive revolution in our own hearts and in the evangelical church, if we are going to start thinking about it and praying for it, we must be realistic. The place to begin is to understand that we live in a post-Christian world. Because man has turned from God, there are hungers on every side. There is death in the *polis*. *There is death in the city.*

Our generation is hungry—hungry for love, for beauty, for meaning. The 'dust of death' covers all. And as in Jeremiah's day, there is with us the unsatisfied longing for a sufficient comforter.

Jeremiah said it well in Lamentations 1:16: 'For these things I weep; mine eye, mine eye runneth down with water, because the comforter that should relieve [bring back] my soul is far from me.' Why did the Jews in Jeremiah's day seek comfort and not find it, seek satisfaction and not find it? Because they had forgotten the end of man, the purpose of man. Often, when talking about the purpose of man, we quote from the first answer of the Westminster Catechism: 'Man's chief end is to glorify God'—and the sentence is ended there. This completely changes our Reformation forefathers' understanding of the Scriptures. If you are going to give the complete biblical answer you must finish their sentence: 'Man's chief end is to glorify God, *and to enjoy him for ever.*' That changes the whole view of life.

Our calling is to enjoy God as well as to glorify Him. Real fulfilment relates to the purpose for which we were made, to be in reference to God, to be in personal relationship with Him, to be fulfilled by Him, and thus to have an affirmation of life. Christianity should never give any onlooker the right to conclude that Christianity believes in the negation of life. Christianity is able to make a real affirmation because we affirm that it is possible to be in personal relationship to the personal God who is there and who is the final environment of all He created. All else but God is dependent, but being in the image of God, man can be in personal relationship to that which is ultimate and has always been. We can be fulfilled in the highest level of our personality and in all the parts and portions of life.

There is nothing Platonic in Christianity. It is not the soul alone that is to be fulfilled and the body and the intellect to be minimized. There does exist an intellectualism which is destructive to Christianity, but that is not true Christian intellectual comprehension. The whole man is to be fulfilled; there is to be an affirmation of life that is filled with joy. Only too often when we look at Christians, we do not find the excitement that Christianity should bring in their lives. We do not find them being fulfilled in *the whole man* in relationship to the God who is there.

And so too in the days of Jeremiah we find that the Jews had turned away from the true fulfilment. However, these ancient Jews were not nearly as badly off as the modern man of our own post-Christian world. They turned to false gods, but at least they still knew something was there. In a similar way the Greeks built their culture. Of course their gods were inadequate, so that, for example, Plato never found what to do with his absolutes because his gods were not big enough. And the Greek writers did not know what to do with the Fates because the gods were not great enough always to control them. But at least they knew something was there. It is only our foolish generation (and I am using 'foolish' in the terms of Romans 1) that lives in a universe which is purely material, everything being reduced to mass, energy and motion. Thus we find that the Jews left the true God for false gods, just as the Greeks, the Romans and others had false gods, but they were not as far from the truth as our generation. Our generation has nobody home in the universe, nobody at all. Let us understand this: in the final analysis only a personal comforter can comfort man who is personal, and only one Comforter is great enough, the infinite-personal God who exists, that is, the God of Judeo-Christian Scripture. Only He is the sufficient Comforter.

The Song of Solomon beautifully depicts the need for a personal comforter. This magnificent love song in the midst of the Bible puts emphasis upon the fact that God has made us man *and* woman. This is why there is a place for a love song in the Scriptures. In the Song of Solomon we find that the girl has gone to her room for the night; she has anointed herself with perfumes and has retired. Then there is a knock at the door. Her lover has come and he wants her to be with him. But she hesitates and remains inside. She has gone to bed and does not want to get up; after all, she has washed and her hands are anointed. Then suddenly he leaves, and as soon as she realizes this, she sees that all the perfume is absolutely worthless once the lover has gone. This is exactly the way it is with man. Struggling with the trappings of personality, man finds that, if there is no-one there to be a real and sufficient lover, if there is no infinite-personal God, then his wrestling with the trappings of personality is futile.

Jeremiah here in Lamentations 1 : 16 turns and speaks this truth to the Jews with total force. He says, of course you are going to be without a Comforter. Of course, because you

23

have turned away from Him. And the One who would be an adequate Comforter to you, to the Jews (and we can say it also to our twentieth century), is not there. So you are like the girl with the perfume on her hands; she has let the lover go, and there is no meaning to the perfume.

In Lamentations 1 : 18, we find that this chain of thought is taken a step further: 'The Lord is righteous; for I have rebelled against his mouth.' The Hebrew word translated 'commandment' in the Authorized Version is really 'mouth'. The idea is not only that God has set up certain commandments which the Jews have broken. The Scripture here is more comprehensive than that; it says the Jews have rebelled against all that God has spoken—the propositional revelation of God in which God tells them the real answers to life, the way to please the God who is there, and the way to be in relationship with Him. The only reason men were in the place where they were in the days of Jeremiah, or are in our own post-Christian world, is that they have turned away from the propositional revelation of God and as such they are under the moral judgment of God. In Romans 1 Paul emphasized that because men knew the truth and turned from it, they are under the wrath of God. God is everywhere, but as the Jews of Jeremiah's day turned away from the revelation of God, they were morally separated from Him. As the people of our generation turn away from the propositional revelation of God, they too are in the place where there is no sufficient Comforter, for they are morally separated from Him.

Then in Lamentations 1 : 19 we read this: 'I called for my lovers, but they deceived me: my priests and mine elders gave up the ghost in the city, while they sought their meat to relieve their souls.' And so we find this thought of relieving the soul, of bringing back the soul, is involved for the third time in the unity of this chain of references in Lamentations 1:11; 1:16; and 1:19.

What is the conclusion as man turns away from the revelation of God and from the true God who is there? From what perspective should we be looking at our post-Christian world? Certainly every Christian should have two reactions to our generation. The first is that we should cry because we watch our culture being destroyed, not only that individual men are lost but that our whole culture is being destroyed as well. The second reaction is that we should be aware that, in so far as the culture was built on biblical Reformation thought, and the generations immediately preceding us have turned from that truth, *there must be death in the city*. We must know there will be.

When Jeremiah says, in Lamentations 1:19, that they gave up the ghost in the city, that there is death in the city, the specific city spoken of is Jerusalem. But the word 'city' may be extended further; it may be compared to the Greek word *polis*, that is, the sociological group or culture. Thus, because God is dealing with a culture that has turned away, Jeremiah has only one thing to say: 'There is death in the city. There is death in the city!' And that was true of Jeremiah's day, and it is true in our day.

I am amazed at the evangelical leaders who have been taken by surprise at the changes that have come in our culture in the last few years. We should have predicted them. There is bound to be death in the city once men turn away from the base upon which our culture was built. The modern artists, the writers, understand that there is death in the city.

De Chirico, in his surrealistic paintings, saw the city, the

25

modern culture, to be this way. In his paintings there are great cities, high towers, shadows, statues, puffing trains, but hardly a human being. The full force of what this meant dawned on me a few years ago when I was travelling by train in Europe. In the first-class carriages there are nice coloured pictures. In the second-class carriages there are uncoloured pictures. I had an uncoloured picture. In my carriage was a photograph of a city, the old city of Geneva. There were the streets that I knew very well. But suddenly I saw that in this photograph there was nobody in the city, and I had a weird sensation of death. Then I understood what De Chirico was painting. In our generation there is death in the city.

What kind of death? Are people disappearing? No, we have, if anything, too many people. Rather, it is the death of man. Personality is gone. We are reminded of American artists such as Edward Hopper who also painted that awful, terrible loneliness. Or we recall Nevil Shute's *On the Beach* which pictured the world after the bombs have fallen and men have died. The scene is powerful: the lights are still burning; the generators are still running, but there's nobody there. It's an awful loneliness that Shute builds. But what he is saying is something more profound than that we live in an age of potential nuclear destruction. He is saying, 'Don't you understand? This is where man really is today, whether the bombs fall or not, because there's no final purpose to his existence.' There is death in the city of man. And if we are really alive to the issues of our own day we should at least understand as well as the unbelieving poets, writers, painters and the others that this is the real dilemma: there is death in the city—death in the city of man.

What should we say about our country? Of course, we

should be glad for the freedoms we do have. But, having said that, should we not also understand that since our culture no longer has a Christian base, there is going to be death in the city? Do you think our country can remain as it has been, after it has thrown away the Christian base? Do not be foolish. Jeremiah would have looked at you and said, 'You do not have the correct perspective. You should be crying. Because it is going to be this way. Having turned from the One who can fulfil, the One who can give comfort, having turned away from His love, His propositional revelation, there will be death in *your* city, in *your* culture!' Modern man stands in that place. We see, therefore, that Jeremiah does give us the perspective we should have for our own day. This is his message. History, indeed, is not just mechanical. In Jeremiah's day God worked into history upon the basis of *His character*, and He continues to do so. Those people were going off into the Babylonian captivity not just for military or economic reasons. God, as a holy God, judged them as they had turned away from Him. He will do the same in our generation.

This is the perspective that God's Word gives us. Being Christian means affirming certain doctrines, but it also means having a mentality attuned to what God has shown us in His book about the realities of history. And this must be my perspective, for only as men turn back to the One who can really fulfil, return to His revelation, and reaffirm the possibility of having a relationship with Him as He has provided the way through Jesus Christ, can they have the sufficient comfort which every man longs for. There *is* no other way. And if we are not totally convinced that there is *no* other way, we are not ready for a reformation and revival. We are not ready for the revolution that will shake the evangelical church. If I think there are other final answers in the areas of art, history, psychology, sociology, philosophy, or whatever my subject and whatever my discipline; if I think there are other answers after man has turned away from God; if I think that they are more than temporary, small answers; I am not ready for the reformation, the revival and the revolution—the constructive revolution—which the evangelical church so desperately needs. Our perspective must be the perspective of the Word of God. If it is, then we will offer no cheap solutions; and we will not be surprised that there is judgment.

3 THE MESSAGE OF JUDGMENT

As we have seen, Jeremiah was speaking to an age very much like our own. He is called the 'weeping prophet', for we find him crying over his people. And his attitude must be ours: we must weep over the church as it has turned away and weep over the culture that has followed it.

Jeremiah himself was born in Anathoth, a village just north of Jerusalem, and he died probably in his early sixties in Egypt. He did not have an easy life. In Hebrews 11:36, 37 we read 'And others had trial of cruel mockings and scourgings, yea, moreover of bonds and imprisonment: They were stoned, they were sawn asunder.' As you investigate, you can locate certain people in the Bible who went through all but one of the persecutions outlined in Hebrews 11. You do not find anybody who was sawn asunder. Tradition, however, tells us that after the Jewish nation was taken over by the Babylonians, some of the Jews carried Jeremiah down into Egypt, precisely where he did not want to go and where he told them not to go. The tradition (which may or may not be true) goes further and says that they put him in a hollow log and sawed through it. This might be what the writer of Hebrews is referring to. In any case, Jeremiah's life, which we will look at in more detail, was not an easy one.

His message was not an easy one either. We learn what that basic message was in Jeremiah 1:10: 'See, I have this day set thee over the nations and over the kingdoms, to root out, and to pull down, and to destroy, and to throw down, to build, and to plant.' Notice the order. First, there was to be a strong negative message—and then the positive one. But the negative message was primary. It was to be a message of judgment to the church which had turned away and to the culture which flowed from it. Judah had revolted against God and His revealed truth; and God says that Jeremiah's message was to be basically a message of judgment. I believe the same message is to be ours today.

Christianity is not romantic, not soft. It is tough-fibred and realistic. And the Bible gives us the realistic message that Jeremiah preached into his own day, a message I am convinced the church today must preach if it is to be any help in the post-Christian world.

Let us not be surprised at the world's reaction. The Bible makes it plain that this message is going to be poorly received by a church and by a culture in revolt. We read in Jeremiah 1:18, 19, 'For, behold, I have made thee this day a defenced city, and an iron pillar, and brasen walls against the whole land, against the kings of Judah, against the princes thereof, against the priests thereof, and against the people of the land. And they shall fight against thee; but they shall not prevail against thee; for I am with thee, saith the Lord, to deliver thee.' In other words, God says, 'This is the type of ministry you are going to have, Jeremiah.' So if you are a Christian looking for an easy ministry in a post-Christian culture where Christians are a minority, you are unrealistic in your outlook. It was not to be so in Jeremiah's day, and it *cannot* be so in a day like our own.

Jeremiah then turns to analyse the various ways in which his culture was turning away from God. He focuses on a number of faults: the inadequacy of a merely external religion, the general apostasy of the church, a few specific sins, and the tendency to search for meaning and security apart from the God who is there.

Jeremiah points out that although there was plenty of external religion, that was not what God wanted. We read, for example, in Jeremiah 6:20, 'To what purpose cometh there to me incense from Sheba, and the sweet cane from a far country? Your burnt-offerings are not acceptable, nor your sacrifices sweet unto me.' There was plenty of sacrifice, but it was no good. They were functioning in the wrong way with the wrong motivation and the wrong propositions. So God said, 'What good is your religion to me?' The point is the same in Jeremiah 7:4: 'Trust ye not in lying words, saying, The temple of the Lord, The temple of the Lord, The temple of the Lord.' In other words the people said, 'Is not the temple of the Lord with us? Then all will be well!' But God brought down His hands in anger and said, 'I do not care anything about your temple once you have turned away from my revealed truth. Once you have done this, you can have the temple there, but it does not mean a thing to me.'

So it is in our own generation. The fact that there is much religion means nothing to God and does nothing to remove His judgment. The new theology or the compromises that one finds sometimes even in some so-called evangelical-ism remove the real thing that makes religion acceptable to God. As we saw in Lamentations, the Jews had turned away from the revelation of God, and when men turn away from the propositional revelation of God, it destroys the acceptability of their worship to God. We are not jousting over abstract theological terms. We are dealing with a question of believing God and believing His revealed truth.

Jeremiah, however, goes further in 7:10: 'And come and stand before me in this house, which is called by my name, and say, We are delivered to do all these abominations?' That is, 'You come into the temple and then you go away and say, "Now I can do anything I wish. I can live the hedonistic life."' But God says through Jeremiah, 'Not so. Mere external religion means nothing to me.' In 9:25 we find the same emphasis: 'Behold, the days come, saith the Lord, that I will punish all them which are circumcised with the uncircumcised.' They were circumcised, but what did it amount to? Nothing in the sight of God unless it was rooted in the truth of the revelation of God. The external forms alone mean *nothing* to God.

But through Jeremiah, God says more than this. Jeremiah speaks out expressly against apostasy. Here is a hallmark of our generation, one that shows the church today has been infiltrated by the relativism of the Hegelian concept of synthesis: since the thirties more and more the church has ceased to use the word 'apostasy'. It is easy to use the word in a hard and harsh way. That is wrong, of course. Nevertheless, on the basis of the Word of God, there is such a thing as apostasy, and when we see a real turning away from God, we are not faithful to the Word of God unless we call it what it is.

Through Jeremiah God speaks in strong, strict, even shocking terms about it: 'They say, If a man put away his wife, and she go from him, and become another man's, shall he return unto her again? shall not that land be greatly polluted? but thou hast played the harlot with many lovers' (Jeremiah 3:1). And then he gives the invitation, 'Yet return again to me, saith the Lord.' But the invitation is rooted in accepting the fact that what had been done before was real apostasy.

The picture in which the invitation is given is highly significant. Throughout Scripture God continually says, 'You are my bride.' For the church of God to turn away is spiritual adultery, *apostasy*. One must be careful not to use the word proudly, harshly, without love, without tears; but there is a proper way. The picture is repeated in Jeremiah 3:6: 'The Lord said also unto me in the days of Josiah the king, Hast thou seen that which backsliding Israel hath done? she is gone up upon every high mountain and under every green tree, and there hath played the harlot.' The Jews were turning away to false gods. But turning away to false theology is equal to turning away to false gods. Whenever the church of Jesus Christ turns away from the living God and His propositional truth, she is playing the harlot. In Jeremiah 3:9 we find the same: 'And it came to pass through the lightness of her whoredom, that she defiled the land, and committed adultery with stones and with stocks.'

Therefore, in a post-Christian world and in an often post-Christian church it is imperative to point out with love where apostasy lies. We must openly discuss with all who will listen, treating all men as fellow men, but we must call apostasy by its proper name. If we do not do that, we are not ready for reformation, revival and a revolutionary church in the power of the Holy Spirit.

We are all too easily infiltrated with relativism and synthesis in our own day. We tend to lack antithesis. There is that which is true God, and there is that which is no god. God is there in opposition to His not being there. That is the big antithesis. And there are antitheses throughout His revelation, from Genesis 1 on. There is that which is given which is antithetical to its opposite. When we see men ignore or pervert the truth of God, we must say clearly—not in hate or anger—'You are wrong'.

Jeremiah not only speaks against religious apostasy, but also against specific sins. This is likewise imperative in a generation such as our own. So God says, in Jeremiah 5:7, 8, 'How shall I pardon thee for this? thy children have forsaken me, and sworn by them that are no gods.' That is the religious side again. But note the effect of the affluent society: 'when I had fed them to the full, they then committed adultery, and assembled themselves by troops in the harlots' houses.' They used their affluence for sin. Does that sound familiar? Consider modern dramas, novels, films, painting, sculpture. In the midst of the affluent society often the artist's answer is a call to the hedonistic life.

Jeremiah continues in 5:8: 'They were as fed horses in the morning.' If a horse is well fed, says Jeremiah, it turns to sexual things. So he says that is the way you are in your affluent society, O Jews. And that is the way you are, O affluent United States and northern European Reformation countries, turning from the Reformation faith. 'They are as fed horses in the morning: every one neighed after his neighbour's wife.' Think of the novels today, such as John Updike's *The Couples*, which express this escape into an adulterous community. Many young people say to me, 'Why shouldn't I take to drugs when the generation before me finds its escape in alcohol and adultery?' They are completely right. One is as bad as the other. It will not do for a society that lives on adultery and alcohol to turn then to those who would carry it a step further and act as though there is a qualitative difference between the two. There is only a quantitative difference. The church which does not speak of the sins of the last generation is in no position to speak against the sins of this generation.

When the church does not speak against sin in the post-Christian world, it does not follow God's example through Jeremiah as to what its message should include. External religion, apostasy, sexual sins—and lying. That too Jeremiah speaks about. In Jeremiah 9:2 we read, 'Oh that I had in the wilderness a lodging place of wayfaring men; that I might leave my people, and go from them! for they be all adulterers, an assembly of treacherous men.' And in the fifth verse, 'And they will deceive every one his neighbour, and will not speak the truth: they have taught their tongue to speak lies, and weary themselves to commit iniquity.' God is also concerned about men speaking truth.

Men no longer believe that there are absolutes, and more and more it has become the accepted thing not to speak the truth. The business contract is not honoured if a way can be legally found around it. The employer does not honour his promise. The employee responds in kind. As men have turned away from God, who alone gives a basis for absolutes in truth, men have become untruthful and hypocritical with each other.

The phrase 'a plastic culture' relates well to this. It fits. Ours is a plastic culture, and often ours is a plastic church. Men are simply carrying on by memory. They are living only by habit, not because they have a firm, rational, Christian base for their actions, and it is indeed ugly. It is so easy to see this hypocrisy and ugliness in both culture and church that we should not have had to wait for the present generation to tell us. The church should have been saying this for years. The beauty is gone if we continue to do even the right things once the base which produced these is gone.

We live in a day when truth is worn down in the philosophy of our generation. This is so not just in the chairs of philosophy, but in the places where living philosophy is being beaten out now, and we cannot expect truth to be torn down either in the university or in the arts without a result in the practice of society.

But Jeremiah speaks for God and says, 'I'm not only speaking against sexual sin; I'm speaking about cutting down the force of truth.' In 9:8 he says, 'Their tongue is as an arrow shot out; it speaketh deceit: one speaketh peaceably to his neighbour with his mouth, but in heart he layeth his wait.' It is easy for both the orthodox and the liberal church to talk of love and yet live without it. And it is easy for the modern generation outside the church to do the same. The hippies, too, often use the word love, but they have left Haight-Ashbury a desert. Drawn by the cry of 'love', many a flower child has been exploited and sucked empty for life by the time she is fourteen. Both inside the church and outside the church to use the word 'love' and other peaceable words in order to deceive is simply exploitation.

God spoke to Jeremiah against such falsehood and exploitation. And if the church is not speaking in strong terms against both the apostasy and the sins of our own day, we are not ready to see any sort of revolutionary movement into a tough generation. Our generation is properly sick of god-words.

Jeremiah also speaks against looking to the world for help. In his day this was very specific. It was looking to

Egypt and other great nations for protection against Baby-lon. In 2:18 we find Jeremiah saying, 'And now what hast thou to do in the way of Egypt, to drink the waters of Sihor? or what hast thou to do in the way of Assyria, to drink the waters of the river?' That is, 'What are you doing looking to Egypt? What are you doing looking to Assyria? Why don't you look to God?' For Jeremiah it was a literal Egypt. Our Egypt is the world and the world's cleverness. We cannot expect a tough generation sick and tired of the glib and the plastic to take the church seriously if it uses the world's way. As Jeremiah says in 2:36, 'Why gaddest thou about so much to change thy way? thou also shalt be ashamed of Egypt, as thou wast ashamed of Assyria.'

Or again in 37:7, 8, Jeremiah says, 'Thus saith the Lord, the God of Israel; Thus shall ye say to the king of Judah, that sent you unto me to inquire of me; Behold, Pharaoh's army, which is come forth to help you, shall return to Egypt into their own land. And the Chaldeans shall come again, and fight against this city, and take it, and burn it with fire.'

'Are you looking to the world for help?' God asks. It is going to fail. You are going to be ashamed. The church that says there is truth in a generation of relativism, a church that says God is there, when the new theology turns religion into mere psychology—such a church must demonstrate that it really believes God is there. We must look directly to God for help. As Hudson Taylor used to say, it must be the Lord's work done in the Lord's way.

So what then is the message Jeremiah gave to the Jews? Was it a light message? What he said was, 'You are going on to utter destruction because you have turned away from God and because you will not repent. The God who works in history is going to bring upon your culture utter destruction.' And so he writes in 1:14, 'Then the Lord said unto me, Out of the north an evil shall break forth upon all the inhabitants of the land.' And in 5:15, 'Lo, I will bring a nation upon you from far, O house of Israel, saith the Lord: it is a mighty nation, it is an ancient nation, a nation whose language thou knowest not, neither understandest what they say.' The whole book is full of such prophecy. Utter destruction is coming upon your whole culture, utter destruction.

What we need are new John Bunyans to point out what occurs when men turn to Vanity Fair. When men turn away from God, the city becomes the city of destruction. In 9:11, 'And I will make Jerusalem heaps, and a den of dragons; and I will make the cities of Judah desolate, without an inhabitant.' In 21:4, 'Thus saith the Lord God of Israel; Behold, I will turn back the weapons of war that are in your hands.' To our generation God says, 'O nation, O culture, do you think because of the knowledge you now have, a knowledge that is separated from what is really there (the universe in which there is a supernatural as well as a natural, in which everything is not merely economic cause and effect), do you think you can build weapons that will meet your need? No,' says God, 'these things are going to turn as a sword in a weak man's hand, and it is going to cut the man who holds it. You are trusting in increased technology. The technology will destroy you.' Until we hear men preaching with this kind of contemporary courage, we cannot expect the church to be taken seriously.

'I will turn back the weapons of war that are in your hands, wherewith ye fight against the king of Babylon, and against the Chaldeans, which besiege you without the walls, and I will assemble them into the midst of this city. And I myself will fight against you with an outstretched hand and with a strong arm, even in anger, and in fury, and in great wrath. And I will smite the inhabitants of this city, both man and beast: they shall die of a great pestilence. And afterward saith the Lord, I will deliver Zedekiah king of Judah, and his servants, and the people, and such as are left in this city from the pestilence, from the sword, and from the famine, into the hand of Nebuchadrezzar' (Jeremiah 21:4-7).

Our generation needs to be told that man cannot disregard God, that a culture like ours that has had such light and then has deliberately turned away stands under God's judgment. God is a God of grace, but the other side of the coin of grace is judgment. If God is there, if God is holy (and we need a holy God or we have no absolutes), there must be judgment.

Do you really believe He is there? Why is there so much unreality among evangelicals, young and old? What is the final reality? The final reality is that God is really there. The Bible is what it is because the God who exists has spoken it in propositional, verbalized form. But does *your* Christianity end with something less than God who is there? In your learning, your teaching, your living, do you believe He is there? Do you *really* believe He is there, or are you only living in some sort of sociological belief? If He is really there and if He is a holy God, do you seriously think that God does not care that a country like our own has turned from Him? There is only one kind of preaching that will do in a generation like ours—preaching which includes the preaching of the judgment of God.

In the last chapter, we looked at the way Jeremiah spoke God's word to his own age. We saw how he preached judgment against a merely external religion, against the general apostasy, and against specific sins—adultery, lying and hypocrisy. Jeremiah's voice was raised against the travesty his own people had made of God's revealed truth.

We turn now to examine not so much the sins of the people as the people themselves. To whom was Jeremiah speaking? Was it just the ordinary people in the next village? Whom did he accuse of turning away from God?

In Jeremiah 22:11, 12 we read, 'For thus saith the Lord touching Shallum the son of Josiah king of Judah, which reigned instead of Josiah his father, which went forth out of this place; He shall not return thither any more: but he shall die in the place whither they have led him captive, and shall see this land no more.' Here we find immediately the preaching of an utter destruction which includes the king of the land. Jeremiah 22:18, 19 has the same emphasis: 'Therefore thus saith the Lord concerning Jehoiakim the son of Josiah king of Judah; They shall not lament for him, saying, Ah my brother! or, Ah sister! they shall not lament for him, saying Ah lord! or, Ah his glory! He shall be buried with the burial of an ass, drawn and cast forth beyond the gates of Jerusalem.'

Thus Jeremiah speaks soberly, using a very strong figure of speech. The judgment of God is coming upon this land as men have turned so far from Him that, rather than having the glorious funeral which the kings of Judah wanted to have, this king would be buried like an ass. How do you bury an ass? You drag him outside the city, abandon his carcass, and that's that. Such is the kind of judgment that is coming from God upon the generation that has turned away. Again in 25:9-11 we feel the emphasis of utter destruction: 'Behold, I will send and take all the families of the north, saith the Lord, and Nebuchadrezzar the king of Babylon, my servant, and will bring them against this land, and against the inhabitants thereof, and against all these nations round about, and will utterly destroy them, and make them an astonishment, and an hissing, and perpetual desolations. Moreover I will take from them the voice of mirth. . . .' Jeremiah's generation was seeking everywhere for the voice of mirth, even where there was no real mirth. And God says, 'I am going to take away from them the voice of mirth. What am I going to use as an instrument? I am going to use a nation that is not my people, a military force that is not following the living God, and I am going to use them against *you*.'

I must say that when I pray for my country and our culture, I do not pray for God's justice. I can only plead for His mercy. If we had the justice of God, we would not have peace. We would have a situation like Jeremiah's. How dare we pray for justice upon our culture when we have so deliberately turned away from God and His revelation?

Why should God bless us? Jeremiah was counted a traitor because he spoke like this, but it is what God put in his mouth: 'Yes, you're the people of God; yes, externally you seem to have the real religion in the temple, but it's worth nothing to me, and because you have turned from me and from the propositional truth that I have given you, I am going to send an overwhelming judgment upon you.' So for my generation I pray only for one thing—God's mercy. But for Jeremiah's day the message of total destruction goes on: I 'will bring them against this land, and against the inhabitants thereof, and against all these nations round about, and will utterly destroy them, and make them an astonishment, and an hissing, and perpetual desolations. Moreover I will take from them the voice of mirth, and the voice of gladness, the voice of the bridegroom, and the voice of the bride. . . .' The central things of life are going to grind down to a close: 'the sound of the millstones, and the light of the candle', that is, the conduct of business as well as the joy of marriage. 'And this whole land shall be a desolation, and an astonishment; and these nations shall serve the king of Babylon seventy years.' Then, of course, comes that marvellous promise: after seventy years God will return them to the land. But Jeremiah's message to the generation to which he was preaching was destruction.

When Jeremiah preached destruction, he was not just talking in generalities. He preached against the dignitaries, the leaders of the land, who were drawing their people away from God. So we find in Jeremiah 8:1, 'At that time, saith the Lord, they shall bring out the bones of the kings of Judah, and the bones of his princes, and the bones of the priests, and the bones of the prophets, and the bones of the inhabitants of Jerusalem, out of their graves.' That is,

Jeremiah says, 'I'm talking against you, O kings. I'm talking against you, O priests. I'm talking against you, O prophets.' Jeremiah preached against the dignitaries who might have been great in the natural hierarchy of that society and state but who were leading the people astray. He continues this emphasis in 13:13, 14: 'Then shalt thou say unto them, Thus saith the Lord, Behold, I will fill all the inhabitants of this land, even the kings that sit upon David's throne, and the priests, and the prophets, and all the inhabitants of Jerusalem, with drunkenness. And I will dash them one against another, even the fathers and the sons together, saith the Lord.' He names those who are the leaders of the land, who stand in the social and state hierarchy—the kings, the prophets and the priests. We also find a similar message toward the end of the book. (I am almost choosing at random, because the total message of Jeremiah is repeated over and over again throughout the many years he prophesied.) Thus in Jeremiah 34:19, 20: 'The princes of Judah, and the princes of Jerusalem, the eunuchs, and the priests, and all the people of the land, which passed between the parts of the calf [that is, who made a covenant in God's name and then broke it]; I will even give them into the hand of their enemies, and into the hand of them that seek their life: and their dead bodies shall be for meat unto the fowls of the heaven, and to the beasts of the earth.' It is easy to preach like this to the common people, but what Jeremiah did under the moving of God was to have the courage to vocalize and to verbalize the preaching of God against the dignitaries who could do something about it. He even dared to name them. He dared to say, '*You* are leading us astray, and God's judgment is upon *you*.' Naturally, as in our own day, such preaching brings a repercussion from those in power in either the church or state.

Jeremiah did not just preach against the political dignitaries, but, more than anyone else, against the religious leaders who were leading the people away from the propositional revelation of God. In Jeremiah 2:8 he says, 'The priests said not, Where is the Lord? and they that handle the law knew me not: the pastors also transgressed against me, and the prophets prophesied by Baal, and walked after things that do not profit.'

And so he turns here and asks, 'The religious leaders, are they leading you aright?'

And he says, 'No.'

'Are they to be honoured merely because they're religious leaders?'

'Not if they're not preaching that which is truth.'

Surely this has something to do with the message we must speak to our post-Christian world. We must treat men with love, we must treat them and talk to them humanly. But we must not tone down our message: the religious leaders of our day too are leading people astray. There is nothing in the Bible that removes a man from under the judgment of Scripture just because he is a religious leader. In fact, it is the other way around.

Further, we find in Jeremiah 5:13, 'And the prophets shall become wind, and the word is not in them: thus shall it be done unto them.' What's the matter with the prophets? The trouble is they are not speaking for God. They are merely taking the social consensus of their day and speaking as though that was the Word of God. In verse 31, 'The prophets prophesy falsely, and the priests bear rule by their means; and my people love to have it so: and what will ye

44

do in the end thereof?' What of these priests? What of these prophets? They merely echo what everyone around them is saying. Surely that sounds familiar. When we listen to the religion that is largely preached in our generation, we hear the same thing the unbelieving philosophers and sociologists are saying. The only difference is that theological language is used. But God says, 'It will not do. This brings you under my judgment.'

In Jeremiah 12:10 God gives us a graphic picture of the destruction the religious leaders have brought on the people: 'Many pastors have destroyed my vineyard, they have trodden my portion underfoot, they have made my pleasant portion a desolate wilderness.' The religious leaders have walked through God's garden and destroyed it. In Switzerland, every blade of grass is precious; you dare not walk through any field. It would be like walking through someone's rose garden. But here is God's field and someone has trampled down the grass. Is it the common man? No, not primarily. Rather it is the religious leaders who made the garden a desolate, desolate wilderness. Surely then, we cannot fail to speak against the religious leaders, when they are the ones who are bringing the desolation.

In Jeremiah 23:1, the figure of speech changes: 'Woe be unto the pastors that destroy and scatter the sheep of my pasture! saith the Lord.' Walking upon God's garden has now become scattering the sheep. Who scatters the sheep? Again it is the religious leaders. 'Therefore', Jeremiah continues, 'thus saith the Lord God of Israel against the pastors that feed my people; Ye have scattered my flock, and driven them away, and have not visited them: behold, I will visit upon you the evil of your doings, saith the

Lord.' Don't you care for the sheep? Well then I will visit upon you the natural results of what you have taught. Malcolm Muggeridge, as he wrote in *The New Statesman*, 'The Death Wish of the Liberal', saw from his own liberal background exactly where liberalism has led. Removing the absolutes, liberalism has led into a wilderness. It has eliminated the categories that make the difference between love and non-love. It has led us all the way to Antonioni's film *Blow Up*, advertised as 'Murder without guilt, Love without meaning'. But it can lead further. It can lead us into Fellini's film *Juliet of the Spirits*, where men no longer know the distinction between the external world and fantasy. The sheep are scattered.

The sheep are scattered even further than they were by the false prophets of Jeremiah's day. At least the Jews had still some kind of gods, false as they were. Our generation has become so ridden with folly that it lives merely in a materialistic world, shut up finally to the flow of atoms, to the flow of consciousness, contemplating itself without categories and without values. No wonder God says, 'I am going to judge you for what you have done.' Who was responsible for this in Jeremiah's day? The religious leaders. Who has done it in our own? Surely the greatest judgment must be not upon those who have destroyed from the outside. Certainly the greatest guilt rests upon the church which knew the truth, deliberately turned away from it, and now only presents men with relativism, an echo of modern secular thought.

Jeremiah continues in 23: 11: 'For both prophet and priest are profane; yea, in my house have I found their wickedness, saith the Lord.' It is a horrible thing to dwell in wickedness if you're one of God's people. But to bring the wickedness into the house of God is a double sin. And God says, 'Where has this wickedness sprung from? It has sprung from my own house.' Likewise, in our own culture what has cut the ground from under the base was on the inside. In the days of deism in our country, it was indeed true that in places there were few Christians, but rarely did the church itself become deistic. Rather, although the churches may have shrunk in size, when a man entered the church he could hear the truth. But in our generation, when men listen at the doors of many churches, what they hear is non-truth.

Furthermore, we find these words in 23:13-16: 'And I have seen folly in the prophets of Samaria; they prophesied in Baal, and caused my people Israel to err.' That was in the northern kingdom. But now Jeremiah swings around to the southern kingdom, and he says, Are you better? 'I have seen also in the prophets of Jerusalem an horrible thing: they commit adultery, and walk in lies: they strengthen also the hands of evildoers. . . .' What is this? Is it not situational ethics? Jeremiah continues: '. . . that none doth return from his wickedness: they are all of them unto me as Sodom, and the inhabitants thereof as Gomorrah. Therefore thus saith the Lord of hosts concerning the prophets; Behold, I will feed them with wormwood, and make them drink the water of gall: for from the prophets of Jerusalem is profaneness gone forth into all the land.' And verse 21, 'I have not sent these prophets, yet they ran: I have not spoken to them, yet they prophesied.' They have come and spoken in the name of God, and they have said 'God says', but they have not had the Word of God. It has merely been their own words welling up inside themselves and echoing the society which surrounds them. These men come and say 'Here is the message of God', but it is not. It is the message of man.

Do you think God is going to take this lightly? If you believe that a holy God is really there, do you think He can take it lightly when people spread over the face of the earth and move among the people of God, and say 'This is the Word of God' when they are speaking only from themselves and are directly contradicting what God has propositionally revealed? How do you expect God to take it lightly? What is He? Is He really an old man rocking in a chair, blind and hard of hearing?

Once more we read in this same chapter, verse 26: 'How long shall this be in the heart of the prophets that prophesy lies? Yea, they are prophets of the deceit of their own heart.' And finally we read in verse 30, which is especially strong, 'Therefore, behold, I am against the prophets, saith the Lord, that steal my words every one from his neighbour.' What do the prophets say? This prophet hears that prophet, and then he repeats the message. And all you hear are echoes. It is like being in a hollow, boarded-up building: all you hear is echo, echo, echo, echo. Study the theology of our own day and all you hear is the echo, echo, echo, *echo*! Echoing what? Echoing what this man says, what that man says, what materialistic sociology teaches, what materialistic psychology teaches, what materialistic economics teaches, what materialistic philosophy teaches. Echoing, echoing, *echoing* as though the words were sprinkled with holy water because they now repeat these same things in theological terms.

And do you expect God to sit there and just rock in the heavens and say, 'Isn't that nice; isn't that nice; isn't that nice'? What kind of a god do you have? And if such a god

48

existed what kind of a god would he be? What would be the use of having him? People have said that we who are evangelicals believe in a sort of old man with a beard. And we say it is not true, it is not true. But I must say that in looking upon the evangelical church, it seems to me very often we give them the right to say it. And so I would speak to the church, to my own generation, and also to that portion of the evangelical church that is getting wobbly at the edges, and say *God will judge*! If we do not have the courage to say that, and mean it, we cannot expect young people to do more than say god-words, god-words, god-words.

But we come to the worst sin of all. In 6:14 we read, 'They have healed also the hurt of the daughter of my people slightly, saying, Peace, peace; when there is no peace.' The same language is used in Jeremiah 8:9-11. What does it mean? Imagine a bulging wall that is about to fall and somebody comes and only whitewashes it. The prophets are giving just such cheap solutions, says God, healing the hurt of my people slightly, slightly. They were saying, 'It's better than you think. Don't be despondent, don't get disturbed, take it easy, the day is not so bad, don't worry too much, peace, peace.' And God says, 'I hate this above everything else: my people are under my judgment because they have revolted from me, and the prophets who claim to speak for God say peace, peace, when there is no peace.' Near the end of his prophecy, in 27:14, 15, we find him speaking in exactly the same way: 'Therefore hearken not unto the words of the prophets that speak unto you, saying, Ye shall not serve the king of Babylon: for they prophesy a lie unto you.' They were saying, 'Don't worry; Babylon isn't going to take this country. Really it's not going to be so bad; you're going to make it.' And then God said this: 'For I have not sent them, saith the Lord, yet they prophesy a lie in my name.' And so here you have it again—speaking lightly of that which is serious, giving all kinds of secondary solutions.

What caused such a breakdown in *our* culture? The two world wars? Do not believe it. If the house had been strong, it would not have come down with the earthquake. If the heart had not been eaten out of the culture, the world wars would not have broken it. 'Don't worry,' some say, 'it is only a technological problem, and technology will be a solution.' But that is not true. Man would not be in the position he is in simply because of technological problems if he had had a really Christian base. A population explosion? Of course it is serious, but it is not the heart of the problem. The fact that our society is now urban rather than agrarian? Is this the final problem? No. To solve only the urban problem is to heal 'slightly'. You can hear it over and over again—all kinds of secondary solutions to secondary problems. Of course these are problems; but they are not the central problem. And men who use theological language to fasten our eyes upon them as the central problem stand under the judgment of God, because they have forgotten that the real reason we are in such a mess is that we have turned away from the God who is there and the truth which He has revealed. The problem is that the house is so rotten that even smaller earthquakes shake it to the core.

Jeremiah, in 28:1-15, gives us a specific example of a prophet, Hananiah, who said, 'Don't worry, everything is going to go well.' Hananiah prophesied that within two years God would bring back the hostages that had been taken to Babylon. But God, speaking through Jeremiah, said, 'Hananiah, it's not so, and not only not so, but God is going to judge you, because you are telling the people a lie. You're saying it's not going to be so bad when, O people of God,' says Jeremiah, 'the trouble has hardly begun.' It is a serious thing indeed to use the name of God to say that secondary solutions can cure our problems, when the real problem is that people have turned away from God and the truth that He has revealed in verbalized, propositional form concerning Himself.

We must understand that Jeremiah did not only say these things to great men in general. He named them by name: Manasseh the king (chapter 15), Pashur the chief governor in the house of the Lord (chapter 20), Zedekiah the king (chapter 21), Shallum the king, and Jehoiakim the king and Coniah the king (chapter 22), Hananiah the prophet (chapter 28), and Shemaiah as he was in Babylon writing letters back to Palestine (chapter 29). Most of these names appear in the latter portions of his prophecy. As the situation became more serious, Jeremiah did not lessen his message; rather, he began to name the great people by name, saying to them, 'Look at what you have done.'

What then are the results of his message? We have one indication in Anathoth, Jeremiah's home town. 'Therefore thus saith the Lord of the men of Anathoth, that seek thy life, saying, Prophesy not in the name of the Lord, that thou die not by our hand' (11:21). That is, the people of his own town said, 'Jeremiah, if you don't keep quiet, we're going to kill you. We don't want your prophecy of judgment.' The priests, the prophets, and the people violently opposed him. So in Jeremiah 26:8, 'Now it came to pass, when Jeremiah had made an end of speaking all that the Lord had commanded him to speak unto all the people, that the priests and the prophets and all the people took him, saying, Thou shalt surely die.' And in verse 11, 'Then spake the priests and the prophets unto the princes and to all the people, saying, This man is worthy to die; for he hath prophesied against this city, as ye have heard with your ears.' Those who mean to be tellers of the Word of God in a generation like our own must understand that men are going to say, 'You are cutting out the optimism and, therefore, we are going to bring every pressure against you that we can bring.' When a man stands up in communist or other totalitarian countries today and really speaks of the judgment of God, he gets the same treatment as Jeremiah. Even in the West the results are similar. Men say, 'You are against our culture, you are against the unity of our culture, you are against the progress of our culture, you are against the optimism of our culture, and we are going to do what we can against you.' Our culture may do little if we preach only the positive message but if we are faithful and also preach judgment in state or church, the result will be the same as with Jeremiah.

Men have not changed, not one bit. For a man to think that he can preach the Word of God today and not experience the true price of the cross of Christ in the sense of not being accepted by the culture—for a man to think that he can be a teller, whether he be a teacher, a minister, a Christian artist, poet, musician, film-maker or dramatist—any man who thinks he can speak truly of the things of God today into such a culture as our own and not have such words spoken against him is foolish. It is not possible. It is not possible whether one is the teller with his music or with his voice, whether one plays an instrument or speaks out

52

behind a pulpit, whether one writes a book or paints a picture. To think that one can give the Christian message and not have the world with its monolithic, post-Christian culture bear down on us is not to understand the fierceness of the battle in such a day as Jeremiah's or such a day as our own.

In Jeremiah 36:22-24 we find the same thing: the priests, the prophets, the people rise up against the message. 'Now the king sat in the winterhouse in the ninth month: and there was a fire on the hearth burning before him. And it came to pass, that when Jehudi had read three or four leaves, he cut it with the penknife, and cast it into the fire that was on the hearth, until all the roll was consumed in the fire that was on the hearth. Yet they were not afraid.' And Jeremiah is astonished: that they can take the Word of God, cut it up with a knife, cast it into the fire, and burn it until the message is totally consumed! And he says with wonder, 'Yet they were not afraid, nor rent their garments, neither the king, nor any of his servants that heard all these words.'

This is an exact picture of our own generation. Men today do not perhaps burn the Bible, nor does the Roman Catholic Church any longer put it on the index, as it once did. But men destroy it in the form of exegesis; they destroy it in the way they deal with it. They destroy it by not reading it as written in normal literary form, by ignoring historical-grammatical exegesis, by changing the Bible's own perspective of itself as propositional revelation in space and time, in history.

Jeremiah knew that, though they hated him personally, basically they were raising their voices against God who had given the message. In our generation it is the same.

I would say to you who call yourselves Bible-believing Christians, if you see the Word of God mutilated as it is in our day and are not moved to tears and indignation, I wonder if you love God. We should be filled with wonder and amazement that men dare so treat God's Word.

It is well to remember that all this is an extended commentary on Romans 1:21, 22: 'Because that, when they knew God, they glorified him not as God, neither were thankful; but became vain in their reasoning, and their foolish heart was darkened. Professing themselves to be wise, they became fools.' Jeremiah saw men burning up the Word of God, and he said, 'Don't you understand what is going to happen? You are going to be carried away into Babylon. God is going to judge you.' If we as Bible-believing Christians can see God's Word, God's verbalized, propositional communication, treated as much of the church treats it and are not filled with sorrow and indignation and do not cry out, 'But don't you realize the end thereof?'— I just wonder: do we love God? And do we love His Word? Do we really even believe that He exists? If we fight our philosophic battles, our artistic battles, our scientific battles, our battles in sociology, our battles in psychology, our battles in literature, our battles in drama coolly, without emotional involvement, do we really love God? How can we do it without being moved as Jeremiah was moved? How can we speak of judgment and yet not stand like the weeping prophet with tears?

We have already had a glimpse of the personal results to Jeremiah that the preaching of judgment brings. In Anathoth, the people said, 'Keep quiet or we're going to kill you.' The threats to his liberty were not idle, for we read in Jeremiah 20:2, 'Then Pashur smote Jeremiah the prophet, and put him in the stocks that were in the high gate of Benjamin, which was by the house of the Lord.' The first thing they did was to fasten him in the stocks. Poor Jeremiah, who has been preaching faithfully in the midst of this 'post-Christian' culture, finds himself in the stocks. But his punishment did not end there.

The stocks were not enough for him, so they put him in prison. 'For then the king of Babylon's army besieged Jerusalem: and Jeremiah the prophet was shut up in the court of the prison, which was in the king of Judah's house' (Jeremiah 32:2). Just as his prophecy is coming true, just as the king of Babylon is at the doors, just as the false prophets are being proved wrong, Jeremiah is put into prison, the prison that is in the king's house. Those who know the Doge's palace in Venice can picture this, because that palace contained the most important prison. Apparently it was the same here.

Later on in 33:1 Jeremiah is still in prison: 'Moreover the

word of the Lord came unto Jeremiah the second time, while he was yet shut up in the court of the prison.' But even that was not the end. In Jeremiah 37:15, 16, we read, 'Wherefore the princes were wroth with Jeremiah, and smote him, and put him in prison in the house of Jonathan the scribe: for they had made that the prison. When Jeremiah was entered into the dungeon, and into the cells, and Jeremiah had remained there many days. . . .' So they gradually increased the punishment—from the stocks, to a prison, to a dungeon. Finally, as we read Jeremiah 38:4 and 6, every one of us must be moved. For here is a man of flesh and blood, like ourselves, in a historic space-time situation with his own aspirations, and he is carted off and put into a dungeon. And now his very life is threatened: 'Therefore the princes said unto the king, We beseech thee, let this man be put to death: for thus he weakeneth the hands of the men of war that remain in this city.' That is, Jeremiah is not giving an optimistic answer; he is not saying that everything is going to turn out well. He is not saying that there is an easy solution; all we need is a little more technical advance to make the grade. He is cutting down their humanistic optimism, saying that they are under the judgment of God, and thereby weakening the people, undercutting their morale. 'For this man seeketh not the welfare of this people, but the hurt.' Of course it is not true. Jeremiah is wanting their real welfare. He is saying, 'You must be healed of the real disease, which is your revolt against God, and not merely of some superficial, external wound.' But that did not please the dignitaries.

So we read, 'Then Zedekiah the king said, Behold, he is in your hand: for the king is not he that can do anything against you. Then took they Jeremiah, and cast him into the dungeon . . . that was in the court of the prison: and they let down Jeremiah with cords. And in the dungeon there was no water, but mire: so Jeremiah sunk in the mire.' The story would make vivid drama, but it is not merely a piece of theatre. Jeremiah, a man like ourselves, was put into the innermost dungeon where they put a rope around his arms and lowered him down into the mire. As he went down, he must have wondered: 'What are my feet going to touch?' He was not going to drown, but there was mud at the bottom, and as they let him down, he sunk, and he sunk, and he sunk, maybe to his knees, to his waist, to his arm-pits? We do not know, but he was there, there as a result of his faithful preaching of God's judgment to a 'post-Christian' world.

It is no small thing to stick with the message. It is easy to opt out. Both hippies and evangelicals can easily opt out into their own little ghetto, saying nice things to themselves and closing their eyes to the real situation that surrounds them. One can opt out in many ways. But if we really preach the Word of God to a post-Christian world, we must understand that we are likely to end up like Jeremiah.

We must not think that Jeremiah's trials were merely physical. They were psychological as well, for Jeremiah never saw any change in his own lifetime. He knew that seventy years later the people would return, but he did not live to see it. Jeremiah, like every man, lived existentially on the knife edge of time, moment by moment; and like all of us, he lived day by day within the confines of his own lifetime.

Jeremiah was not just a piece of cardboard: he had a psychological life just as we have. How then was he affected?

There were times when Jeremiah stood in discouragement, overwhelmed by preaching the message of God faithfully to this culture and ending up in the stocks, the prison and the dungeon.

In Jeremiah 15:10 we read, 'Woe is me, my mother, that thou hast borne me a man of strife and a man of contention to the whole earth! I have neither lent on usury, nor men have lent to me on usury; yet every one of them doth curse me.' I am glad Jeremiah said that, because I get discouraged too. And if you are being faithful in your preaching and not just opting out, in a culture like ours you too will experience times of discouragement.

And you say, how can a man of God be discouraged? Anybody who asks that has never been in the midst of the battle; he understands nothing about a real struggle for God. We are real men. We are on this side of the fall. We are not perfect. We have our dreams, our psychological needs, and we want to be fulfilled. There are times of heroism as we stand firm and are faithful in preaching to men who will not listen. But there are also times when we feel overwhelmed.

In Jeremiah 20:14-18, we read one of the great cries of discouragement in the Bible, parallel to some of the cries of Job. But the intriguing thing is that neither Job, nor Jeremiah, nor David in the Psalms (where David often cried out to God, saying, 'Have you turned away your face forever, O God? Where are you?')—in none of these cases does God reprove His people as long as they do not turn from Him, nor blaspheme Him, nor give up their integrity in their attitude toward Him. There is no contradiction here. It is possible to be faithful to God and yet to be overwhelmed with discouragement as we face the world. In fact, if we are never overwhelmed, I wonder if we are fighting the battle with compassion and reality, or whether we are jousting with paper swords against paper windmills.

So Jeremiah says in 20: 14-18, 'Cursed be the day wherein I was born: let not the day wherein my mother bare me be blessed. Cursed be the man who brought tidings to my father, saying, A man child is born unto thee; making him very glad. And let that man be as the cities which the Lord overthrew, and repented not: and let him hear the cry in the morning, and the shouting at noontide; because he slew me not from the womb; or that my mother might have been my grave, and her womb to be always great with me. Wherefore came I forth out of the womb to see labour and sorrow, that my days should be consumed with shame?' Jeremiah was discouraged because he was a man standing against a flood. And nobody who is fighting the battle in our own generation can float on a Beauty Rest mattress. If you love God and love men and have compassion for them, you will pay a real price psychologically.

So many people seem to think that if the Holy Spirit is working, then the work is easy. Do not believe it! As the Holy Spirit works, a man is consumed. This is the record of the revivals; it is the record of those places in which God has really done something. It is not easy!

As I stand and try to give out a message to the world at the café tables and in the universities, publicly and privately —it costs a price. Often there is discouragement. Many times I say, 'I can't go up the hill once more. I can't do it again.' And what is God's answer? Well, first it is important to know that God does not scold a man when his tiredness comes from his battles and his tears from compassion.

Jeremiah, we recall, was the weeping prophet. This has psychological depth as well as historical meaning. He is really *the man weeping*. But what does God expect of Jeremiah? What does God expect of every man who preaches into a lost age like ours? He simply expects a man to go right on. He does not scold a man for being tired, but neither does He expect him to stop his message because people are against him. Jeremiah proclaimed the message to the very end. He was always against going down to Egypt for help. And, as the captivity came, he could have escaped to Babylon. Instead he stayed with the people of God to keep preaching the message even after the judgment had fallen. His people dragged him down to Egypt, and even there he continued to preach the same message, down in Egypt where he never, never wanted to go.

Jeremiah, then, provides us with an extended study of an era like our own, where men have turned away from God and society has become post-Christian. Now, before returning to the book of Romans with which this book began, we should bring together what we have learnt from Jeremiah.

First, we may say that there is a time, and ours is such a time, when a negative message is needed before anything positive can begin. There must first be the message of judgment, the tearing down. There are times, and Jeremiah's day and ours are such times, when we cannot expect a constructive revolution if we begin by overemphasizing the positive message. People often say to me, What would you do if you met a really modern man on a train and you had just an hour to talk to him about the gospel? I would spend forty-five or fifty minutes on the negative, to show him his real dilemma—to show him that he is more dead than even he thinks he is; that he is not just dead in the twentieth-century meaning of dead (not having significance in this life) but that he is morally dead because he is separated from the God who exists. Then I would take ten or fifteen minutes to tell him the gospel. And I believe this usually is the right way for the truly modern man, for often it takes a long time to bring a man to the place where he understands the negative. And unless he understands what is wrong, he will not be ready to listen to and understand the positive. I believe that much of our evangelistic and personal work today is not clear simply because we are too anxious to get to the answer without having a man realize the real cause of his sickness, which is true moral guilt (and not just psychological guilt feelings) in the presence of God. But the same is true in a culture. If I am going to speak to a culture, such as my culture, the message must be the message of Jeremiah. It must be the same in both private and public discourse.

Secondly, with love we must face squarely the fact that our culture really is under the judgment of God. We must not heal the sickness lightly. We must emphasize the reality. We must proclaim the message with tears and give it with love. Through the work of the Holy Spirit there must be a simultaneous exhibition of God's holiness and His love, as we speak. We cannot shout at them or scream down upon them. They must feel that we are with them, that we are saying that we are both sinners, and they must know that these are not just god-words but that we mean what we say. They must feel in our own attitudes that we know we too are sinners, that we are not innately good because we have been born into a Christian home, attend an evangelical church or take some external sacraments.

There is in all of this a time for tears. It will not do to say these things coldly. Jeremiah cried, and we must cry for the poor lost world, for we are all of one kind. There is of course a sense in which there are two humanities, one saved, one lost. But the Bible also tells us that there is only one humanity; we all have a common ancestor and all have been made in the image of God. So I *must* have tears for my kind. But with the tears the message must be clear: our culture, our country, our churches have walked upon what God has given us, and thus all these *are* under the judgment of God.

It is my experience that giving the realistic message does not turn people off—if they feel real compassion in you. As a matter of fact, it is the other way. The real thinkers, the artists, understand the scream of modern man: 'There is something wrong with my culture. It is a dead end.'

Take, for example, the picture by Edvard Munch in which a man is screaming. Or listen to young people crying, 'It's plastic. Our culture is plastic.' The artists, the poets, the hippies and the yippies are screaming 'Something is wrong'. Modern man knows this, but no-one tells him why. It is up to Christians to do so: to point out what is wrong and to show modern man why he is hung up and why his culture is plastic.

Often Christians, young and old alike, have not faced the facts about their own countries—that they are under the judgment of God. Perhaps that explains why they are often without enthusiasm in their proclamation of the gospel, why they just give the crumbling wall a coat of paint.

Third, we must say that if we believe in truth, we must practise truth. We live in an age of Hegelian synthesis and relativism; men do not believe truth exists. How do we expect a world to take us seriously when we say we believe truth exists and then live in a relativistic way?

I would re-emphasize this by quoting from the last appendix of my book *The God Who is There* (this repeats in a shorter form, 'The Practice of Truth', a speech I gave in Berlin at the Congress on Evangelism.) 'In regard to the first of the principles of which we spoke . . ., *The full doctrinal position of historic Christianity must be clearly maintained*, it would seem to me that the central problem of evangelical orthodoxy in the second half of the twentieth century is the problem of the *practice* of this principle. This is especially so when we take into account the spiritual and intellectual mentality which is dominant in our century. . . . The unity of orthodox or evangelical Christianity should be centred around this emphasis on *truth*. It is always important, but doubly so when we are surrounded by so many for whom the concept of truth, in the sense of antithesis, is considered to be totally unthinkable. . . . Moreover, in an age of synthesis men will not take our protestations of truth seriously unless they see by our actions that we seriously *practice* truth and antithesis in the unity we try to establish and in our activities. . . . Both a clear comprehension of the importance of truth and a clear practice of it, even when it is costly to do so, are imperative if our witness and our evangelism are to be significant in our generation and in the flow of history. . . . In an age of relativity the *practice* of truth when it is costly is the only way to cause the world to take seriously our protestations concerning truth. Cooperation and unity that do not lead to purity of life and purity of doctrine are just as faulty and incomplete as an orthodoxy which does not lead to a concern for, and a reaching out towards, those who are lost. . . . All too often the only antithesis we have exhibited to the world and to our own children has been *talking* about holiness *or* our *talking* about love; rather than the consideration and practice of holiness and love together as truth, in antithesis to what is false in theology, in the church, and the surrounding culture.'

Remember the false prophets in Jeremiah's day saying, 'Peace, peace.' Can you imagine Jeremiah saying to them, 'We are all in one group because we all wear ecclesiastical coloured ties'? I can't; and he did not do it. And I firmly believe that this is one of the things we must understand in our days of desperate need when men no longer believe in truth. We cannot expect them to take seriously our belief in objective truth, if in our practice we indicate only a quantitative difference between all men who are in ecclesiastical structures or who use theological language. I do not mean that we should not have open dialogue with men; my words and practice emphasize that I believe love demands it. But I do mean that we should not give the impression in our practice that just because they are expressed in traditional Christian terminology all religious concepts are on a graduated, quantitative spectrum, that in regard to central doctrine no chasm exists between right and wrong.

Fourth, we must realize that to know the truth and to practise it will be costly. At times the price will be high in terms of your own family relationships. Often there is a tremendous pressure upon young Christians as they face their non-Christian families. But the price is also high in society. You may not get the honour which you covet in the academic world, in the artistic world, in the professional world or even in the business world. The price may be high indeed.

Fifth, we must keep on preaching even if the price is high. There is nothing in the Bible that says we are to stop. The Bible says rather, 'Keep on, keep on'. We may think of Paul as he writes in 2 Corinthians 11:24-28, which we could paraphrase: 'I've been beaten by the Jews, I've been beaten by the Gentiles, I've battled the seas, I've known the wrath of men, and I've known the force of Satan.' Did Paul stop? Paul said, 'No, I want to come to Rome and preach the gospel there as well.'

When Luther had begun his preaching, he received word about the first Protestant martyrs. Some monks had read his work, turned to his way of thinking, and were burned alive in the Grand Place in Brussels. The spot is still marked where they died. And the story is that when Martin Luther heard about it, he began to walk the floor and he said, 'I can't go on. I can't do it any more. Because of me other men are being killed. I can't go on!' Then as he wrestled with it, he understood that because it was truth, no matter what the cost to himself or anybody else, he must go on. Thank God, Martin Luther marched straight forward—and the Reformation went forward.

Christianity is not a modern success story. It is to be preached with love and tears into the teeth of men, preached without compromise, without regard to the world's concept of success. If there seem to be no results, remember that Jeremiah did not see the results in his day. They came later. If there seem to be no results, it does not change God's imperative. It is simply up to us to go on, go on, go on, go on, whether we see the results or whether we don't. If you are not willing to go on, you have to ask yourself the question: Do I really believe Christianity is true or is my Christianity only an 'upper-storey' religious concept?

Our day is not totally unique. Time after time Christian cultures have thrown themselves away. Take, for example, the church of the apostle Thomas in India. It began to whittle away at the truth. So the church largely died. There are two ways to bring about such death: one is to compromise the truth and the other to have a dead orthodoxy. Both can equally grind down and destroy the message of a church in a generation, especially if the generation is hard. Do we realize that in China at about the year AD 800 there were Christian churches in almost every single great city? Do we realize that there were hundreds of Christians in the Arabian peninsula just before Mohammed in AD 550? Why was it that Mohammedanism was able to rush over that country? Because of military force? No. When Mohammed came forward and looked at the Christians he said, 'There's nothing here.' And he was largely right. Mohammedanism started and swept that portion of the world. The same thing was true with the church in North Africa, and the primitive church in Armenia, in Georgia, in Gaul. In each of these places there was a Christian church and a growing Christian culture but the church collapsed. The pattern is clear: defection and then destruction.

And we as Christians today, what are we saying? We are saying that we want reformation and we want revival, but still we are not preaching down into this generation, stating the negative things that are necessary. If there is to be a constructive revolution in the orthodox, evangelical church, then like Jeremiah we must speak of the judgment of individual men great and small, of the church, the state, and the culture, for they have known the truth of God and

66

have turned away from Him and His propositional revelation. God exists, He is holy, and we must know that there will be judgment. And like Jeremiah we must keep on so speaking regardless of the cost to ourselves.

The world is lost. The God of the Bible *does* exist. The world is *lost*, but truth is truth. So we cannot but keep on, keep on and still keep on.

6 THE SIGNIFICANCE OF MAN

This book began with Romans 1:21, 22, verses which tell us why man is in the dilemma he is in. Man knew the truth and yet deliberately turned away. We have seen how our generation has turned away in the last few decades, and then compared our age with Jeremiah's in order to show what sort of message we as Christians must speak into our twentieth-century post-Christian world.

Now we must return to the analysis of Romans, beginning by looking again at those early verses, Romans 1:21, 22, for what we must see now is how the Bible considers man himself—his nature and his significance.

Increasingly educated, twentieth-century men tend to emphasize some sort of determinism. Usually it is one of two kinds: chemical determinism (such as the Marquis de Sade put forward and as Francis Crick maintains today) or psychological determinism (such as that emphasized by Freud and those who follow him). In the former, man is a pawn of chemical forces. In the latter, every decision that a man makes is already determined on the basis of what has occurred to him in the past. So whether it is chemical determinism or psychological determinism, man is no longer responsible for what he is or does, nor can he be active in making significant history. Man now is no more than part of a cosmic machine.

The Bible's view of man could not be more different. Romans 1:21, 22 says, 'When they knew God, they glorified him not as God, neither were thankful; but became vain in their reasoning, and their foolish heart was darkened. Professing themselves to be wise, they became fools.' The whole emphasis of these verses is that man has known the truth and deliberately turned away from it. But if that is so, then man is wonderful: he can really influence significant history. Since God has made man in His own image, man is not caught in the wheels of determinism. Rather man is so great that he can influence history for himself and for others, for this life and the life to come.

I am convinced that one of the great weaknesses in evangelical preaching in the last few years is that we have lost sight of the biblical fact that man is wonderful. We have seen the unbiblical humanism which surrounds us, and, to resist this in our emphasis on man's lostness, we have tended to reduce man to a zero. Man is indeed lost, but that does not mean he is nothing. We *must* resist humanism, but to make man a zero is neither the right way nor the best way to resist it. You can emphasize that man is totally lost and still have the biblical answer that man is really great. In fact, only the biblical position produces a real and proper 'humanism'. Naturalistic humanism leads to a diminishing of man and eventually to a zeroing of man. But the Christian position is that man is made in the image of God and, even though he is now a sinner, he can do those things that are tremendous—he can influence history for this life and the life to come, for himself and for others.

Consequently, man's actions are not a piece of theatre,

not just a play. If you see a play one night and then you see it the next night, you know the ending is going to be the same because it is the same play. You see it the third night, and it is the same again. The actions of the characters are a piece of theatre; they are not open to change. But the Bible's emphasis is that man is responsible; his choices influence history. Even sin is not nothingness. Romans 1:21, 22 implies the greatness of man.

Perhaps a new figure of speech will help. Imagine history, space-time history, as feminine, and ourselves, men and women, as masculine. As masculine figures, we can impregnate history. We can plant into it seeds that come to fruition in the external world. Just as a man can impregnate that which brings forth legitimate children or illegitimate children, so the Bible stresses that man is able to impregnate history with either that which is good or that which is bad.

In short, therefore, man is not a cog in a machine; he is not a piece of theatre; he really can influence history. From the biblical viewpoint, *man is lost, but great*.

We could spend a long time on this point because it is crucial to our discussion with twentieth-century people to make plain that Christianity does not destroy the meaningfulness of a man. In fact, it is the only system which gives a final and sufficient meaning to man. Man can influence history even if often, unhappily, that influence in history is not good.

Let us notice that Romans 1:21 says something else. It tells us how men begin to move when they know the true God. Those of us who are Christians, true Bible-believing Christians, may take it as a warning to ourselves: 'When they knew God, they glorified him not as God, neither gave thanks.' And I am convinced with all my heart that the first step in God's people turning away from Him—even while they tenaciously and aggressively defend the orthodox position—is ceasing to be in relationship with Him with a thankful heart. Therefore, as we read this as Christians, though the central thrust is why man is in the position he is, it must also speak to us. Let us be careful—we who stand for the orthodox, historic Christian faith in the twentieth century—that we have a thankful heart. Otherwise it will not be many years until the orthodoxy is gone and we are faced with heterodoxy.

God through Paul puts Romans 1:21 into a very carefully reasoned setting. As a matter of fact, the first eight chapters of the book of Romans are the most systematic presentation of the Christian position in the New Testament. It is my theory that the reason the first eight chapters of Romans make a unity within the unity of the whole book of Romans is that they present Paul's basic message into the Greek and Roman world. Romans is the only book written by Paul to a church he had not visited. When he wrote to Ephesus or Corinth, Paul could assume they already had this basic message because he had preached it to them. But when he wrote to Rome, where he had not preached, he first carefully presented the total structure of the Christian position. Then, of course, he added to it the later chapters. The Greek and Roman world is not very distant from our own world in its intellectual setting. It was a world of thinkers, a highly developed world, such as our own. And we can see here what Paul preached and what Paul thought men have to know if they are to understand true Christianity.

The first eight chapters are divided into a very orderly sequence. Romans 1:1-15 is the introduction, and 1:16, 17 is the theme of all the rest: 'For I am not ashamed of the gospel of Christ: for it is the power of God [the *dynamis* of God, the root of our word *dynamite*] unto salvation to every one that believeth; to the Jew first, and also to the Greek. For therein is the righteousness of God revealed from faith to faith: as it is written, The just shall live by faith.' Here Paul sets forth the theme of the Christian message. And Romans 1:18 to 8:39 is a running, full exegesis of these two verses.

This exegesis is divided into several sections. First is the need of salvation (1:18 – 3:20). And, as we have seen, there is a necessary negative before men are ready to listen to a positive. Second is justification (3:21 – 4:25). So far Paul is talking about how to become a Christian. In the third section he assumes his readers are believers and talks about sanctification in the Christian life, and this is of course, related to our theme of reformation and specifically to revival (5:1 – 8:17). Fourth is glorification, touching on the things in the future (8:18-25). Lastly, 8:26-39 tells us that eternal life is for-ever. Here, then, is a very closely argued structure.

Very often men who must travel a great deal have a basic message which they adapt as they move. I think this was true of Jesus. I believe Jesus gave His teaching many times over. That is at least one of the explanations for the slight differences in the various Gospel accounts. He simply gave the same message in a slightly different way for each slightly different situation. If you had followed Paul, I think you would have heard him giving the same basic message over and over again in order that the gospel would have sufficient content. In fact, wherever there has been great preaching and great evangelizing, it has always stressed a sufficient content. People cannot be saved without it. Those who study Marshall McLuhan might say it this way: It's not enough to have a cool communication; you must have a hot communication: Christianity must be communicated with sufficient content. Consequently, we find that Paul was careful to give sufficient information to those to whom he was preaching.

Now let us notice further this phrase from verse 16: 'For I am not ashamed of the gospel.' In Romans 1:16 and 5:5 Paul is playing upon the word 'ashamed'. In chapter 5 Paul, talking to Christians, writes, 'And hope maketh not ashamed; because the love of God is shed abroad in our hearts by the Holy Spirit which is given unto us.' Paul says that in experience, after you are a Christian, you will not be ashamed. But in 1:16 he is addressing those who are not yet Christians and is saying that he—Paul the preacher, Paul the educated man—was not ashamed of the *system* of the gospel, the *system* of truth, the content of the gospel, as he presented it to the minds of men in the educated Greek and Roman world. He was *not ashamed*, because it gives the answers, the answers that nothing else gives.

We today will not be able to speak out with confidence unless we understand that we need not be ashamed of the gospel and the *answers* it gives to men. If we do not have this confidence, men will feel our defensiveness, and it will not commend the gospel to them. It is just such intellectual defensiveness in preaching the gospel in the educated world that diminishes its effect. But Paul says, 'I'm not ashamed when I stand on Mars Hill, because I have answers that the Greek philosopher does not have. I am not ashamed in the rough and tumble of the market place because I know that the Bible is going to give me the true answers that men need and that nothing else gives.'

Sadly enough, there is a kind of an anti-intellectualism among many Christians: spirituality is falsely pitted against intellectual comprehension as though they stood in a dichotomy. Such anti-intellectualism cuts away at the very heart of the Christian message. Of course, there is a false intellectualism which does destroy the work of the Holy Spirit. But it does not arise when men wrestle honestly with honest questions and then see that the Bible has the answers. This does not oppose true spirituality. So Paul stands here and says, 'I'm not ashamed. I'm not ashamed of the gospel because it will answer the questions of men, it is the *dynamis* of God unto salvation to everyone who believes, to the Jew first, and also to the Greek.'

When Paul speaks here of salvation, he is not limiting the term to becoming a Christian. The concept of salvation in Scripture is much broader than the concept of justification. Salvation is the whole process that results from the finished work of Jesus Christ as He died in space and time upon the cross. It is justification, wherein our guilt is removed by God's forensic declaration that, since a man has cast himself upon Jesus Christ and is relying on His finished work, his guilt is gone. But salvation is also sanctification (the Christian life) and glorification (that great day when the Lord Jesus Christ returns and the Christian's body is raised). And so what Paul is saying is, 'I am not ashamed of the gospel which is the power of God for the salvation of the whole man, the whole of history, and the whole of our future into eternity.'

Let us understand that true Christianity is not Platonic. Much, however, of what passes for Christianity does have the ring of Platonic thinking in it. Platonism says that the body is bad and is to be despised. The only thing that matters is the soul. But the Bible says God made the whole man, the whole man is to know salvation, and the whole man is to know the Lordship of Jesus Christ. The great teaching of the resurrection of the body is not just abstract doctrine; it stands as a pledge and reminder of a very important and a very hopeful fact. It says God made the whole man. God made man spirit and body and He is interested in both. He made man with an intellect and He is interested in the intellect. He made man with an artistic and creative sense of beauty and He is interested in that. Body, mind, artistic sense: these things are not low; they are high. Of course, they can become wrong if they are put in the wrong perspective, but they are not wrong in themselves. Therefore, since God made the whole man and is interested in the whole man, the salvation which Paul preaches is a salvation which touches the whole man.

Salvation has something to say not only to the individual man but also to the culture. Christianity is individual in the sense that each man must be born again, one at a time. But it is not individualistic. The distinction is important. As God made man, He also made an Eve so that there could be finite, horizontal relationships between two people. And these human relationships are important to God, for 'the power of God unto salvation' is also meant to give an answer to the sociological needs of man, the interplay between two men and more. God is interested in the whole man and also in the culture which flows from men's relationship with each other.

So when Paul is saying that he is not ashamed of the gospel which is the power of God unto salvation, do not think it covers just a small area. It has something to say about every division that has come because of the fall.

From the Christian viewpoint, all the alienations (to use our twentieth-century word) that we find in man have come because of man's historic, space-time fall. First of all, man is separated from God; second, he is separated from himself, thus the psychological problems of life; third, he is separated from other men, thus the sociological problems of life; fourth, he is separated from nature and thus the problems of living in the world, for example, the ecological problems. All these need healing.

No wonder Paul says, 'I'm not ashamed of the gospel intellectually because it is going to have the answers that men need. I am not ashamed of the gospel because it is the power of God unto salvation in every single area; it has answers and meaning for both eternity and now.' The gospel is great. If you are a Christian you should be convinced that biblical Christianity is not tawdry; it is not a small thing dealing with a small area of life. If you are not a Christian, you should realize that Christianity is titanic. It speaks to every need of man, not by a leap in the dark but by good and sufficient reasons. In presenting the content of Christianity Paul says there is salvation—justification, sanctification and glorification—for the whole man.

Notice too that Paul says, 'to the Jew first, and also to the Greek'. One of the great marks of the new theology from Karl Barth onward is universalism, the notion that eventually all men are saved. In Barth this universalism is implicit; in those who follow him it is explicit. In Scripture there is no universalism of this type, but there is a universalism of another kind—the teaching that one message fulfils the need of all men. This is true biblical universalism: whether a man is a Jew or a Gentile, whether he lives in the West or the East, whether he lived in ages gone by or in the present, there is one message that will fulfil, or would have fulfilled, his needs: the message of the gospel of Jesus Christ. Paul speaks to both kinds of men—the Jew (the man with the Bible) and the Greek (the man without the Bible). That is, there is a universal message that is fitting for all men and for their total need.

In verse 17 we read, 'For therein is the righteousness of God revealed from faith to faith: as it is written, The just shall live by faith.' He is quoting, of course, from Habakkuk 2:4. Paul is saying something more than that one is saved by faith. As a matter of fact, one must be careful to understand that phrase itself, for often it is presented so that it is no longer biblical. The *basis* of our salvation is not our faith. Faith is rather the instrument, the empty hands, with which we accept the gift. We are not saved by faith in faith. The basis of our salvation is the finished work of Jesus Christ in space and time. Paul emphasizes this in the third chapter where he says we are saved upon the basis of the work of Jesus Christ. Faith is raising empty hands in accepting the gift.

But if this is true for justification, it is also true for sanctification. And so we not only become Christians by faith, but we live existentially by faith. The word 'existential' may be confusing, but the concept is important enough to warrant some explanation. There are two basic ways to use the term. It may refer to existentialism, a philosophy that says there is no real, or reasonable, meaning to man. This definition is perhaps too simple, but it will do. On the other hand 'existential' refers to moment-by-moment reality. A Christian must reject the philosophy of existentialism, but he must emphasize that which is truly existential, for the Bible does not teach a static situation in which one becomes a Christian and that's it. Rather, it teaches that time is moving, and a relationship to God is important at every given existential moment. Consequently, you do not begin the Christian life by faith and then remain static. You continue to live it by faith. Much of Paul's teaching from Romans 5 on deals with this. The Christian, then, should be the true existentialist, moving upon the knife-edge of time, in every given moment being in relationship with God. Moment-by-moment living by faith is what is taught here.

I have tried to set the stage for the carefully reasoned presentation which Paul makes in Romans 1:18 to 2:16 as he talks to *the man without the Bible*. All men—lost or saved— are great in their significance. Having been made in the image of God, man is magnificent even in ruin. God made man to be responsible for his thoughts and his actions, and man fashions a significant history. This is true of both Christians and non-Christians, both men with the Bible and men without the Bible.

7 THE MAN WITHOUT THE BIBLE

In three different places Paul speaks solely to men without the Bible. The first is in Lystra (Acts 14:15-17) where the message is fragmentary because it was interrupted. The second is on Mars Hill (Acts 17:16-32), where he has a longer speech but one that was also broken off. Third is Romans 1:18 – 2:16, where he can develop his argument at ease. We can see here what he was really saying in all these places, for the other two conform to this early section in Romans.

Here, I believe, is where God gives us the method of preaching to our generation, for our generation is largely made up of men without the Bible. How are you going to start talking to them? Are you going to quote from the Bible even if they do not know anything about it—or if they despise or ignore it or do not know its authority? Paul did not. In this passage from Romans 1:18 to 2:16 he does not once quote from the Old Testament. When he begins to talk to the Jew, however, after 2:17, he does quote from the Scripture, because the Jews knew what the Bible was. But in the first part, where he talks to the Greek, the man without the Bible, he talks to him in a different way. And I repeat: I believe with all my heart that we can learn from this the method of preaching to our generation.

How then, does Paul begin to speak to the man without the Bible? He says this in verse 18: 'For the wrath of God is revealed from heaven against all ungodliness and unrighteousness of men, who hold the truth in unrighteousness.' Many of the new translations read 'hinder the truth', but I think 'hold' in the Authorized Version is the better translation. The first thing Paul says to the man without the Bible is this: 'You're under the wrath of God because you hold the truth in unrighteousness.' Notice that he immediately begins to preach the wrath of God. Think now of this man without the Bible (he is no different then than now). If you merely say what Paul said in verses 16 and 17, 'Here's salvation', he will shrug his shoulders and say, 'Why do I need salvation?' Or if modern man thinks he needs salvation, it will be some twentieth-century psychological salvation. But Paul says, 'No. What you need is moral salvation. You are guilty. You have true guilt in the presence of God.'

Terry Southern, who wrote *Candy* and *The Magic Christian*, has something important to say: in the preface of *Writers in Revolt* he makes a distinction between the communist countries, in which the state has built arbitrary absolutes on the basis of arbitrary law, and the modern West, which has oriented everything psychologically. He has a clever sentence which says that we are the first generation in history to do away with crime. He does not mean there is no crime, but that we no longer call it crime: we explain everything as only psychological. In other words, this is the orienting mark of the Western form of Hegelianism as contrasted to the communist form of Hegelianism. So when modern man (whether he is educated or not) thinks he needs salvation, usually he is not thinking of salvation from moral guilt but rather relief from psychological guilt feelings.

I am convinced that many men who preach the gospel and love the Lord are really misunderstood. People make a 'profession' of salvation, but because they have not understood the message they are not really saved. They feel a psychological need and they want psychological relief, but they do not understand that the Christian message is not talking only about psychological relief (though it includes that) but is talking about true moral guilt in the presence of a holy God who really is there. The real need is salvation from true moral guilt, not just relief from guilt feelings. And I am certain that many men who make a profession go away still unsaved, having not heard one word of the real gospel because they have filtered the message through their own thought forms and their own intellectual framework in which the word 'guilt' equals 'guilt feelings'.

But Paul will not allow this. He speaks immediately of the wrath of God, and anyone who is unwilling to speak of the wrath of God does not understand the Christian faith. We have a great verse telling us how to be saved: 'He that believeth on the Son hath everlasting life' (John 3:36). But you must remember that the end of that verse is also this: 'and he that believeth not the Son shall not see life; but the wrath of God abideth on him.' There is no real preaching of the Christian gospel except in the light of the fact that man is under the wrath of God—the moral wrath of God. So Paul has a reply to the man who shrugs his shoulders and says, 'Why do I need salvation?' His response is this: 'You need salvation because you are under the wrath of God. You have broken God's law.'

We must be careful here, for there is, of course, a very definite false Christian legalism. Paul preaches against it in Galatians. Nevertheless, there is no Christian message without a proper legalism. It is this that demarcates Christian from non-Christian thinking at this point. The non-Christian, in the twentieth century especially, has no legal and moral base. Everything floats in space: a fifty-one per cent vote or some type of right-wing or left-wing totalitarianism must decide what is acceptable, or some form of hedonism must be adopted, because, as Plato understood so well, an absolute is necessary for real morality. Plato never found such an absolute, but he understood the problem and so did the neo-Platonic men of the Renaissance.

But the Bible is clear: there is a moral law of the universe. And that basic law is the character of God Himself. There is no law behind God that binds God. Rather God Himself is the law because He is not a contentless God but a God with a character. His character *is* the law of the universe. When He reveals this character to us in verbalized, propositional form, we have the commands of God for men. Thus there are absolutes and categories; the law which God has revealed and which is based upon His character is final. This is the biblical position.

Therefore, when men break these commands, they are guilty, guilty in the same way as a man is guilty when he breaks the law of the state. When a man sins, he sins against the character of God, and he has moral guilt in the presence of the Great Judge. I know very well that people no longer talk very much in these terms. But it is to our loss. You may wonder if one can say such things to the far-out twentieth-century people with whom I come into contact. I would tell you with all my heart that I could not talk with them if I did not say these things. For in contrast to left-wing or right-wing totalitarianism with its changing arbitrary absolutes and in contrast to modern man's relativistic chaos, the Bible's teaching alone gives moral answers to men.

We are told in this eighteenth verse that the man without the Bible holds the truth in unrighteousness. Or if you choose, you can say, he 'hinders' or 'suppresses' the truth. I will deal later with the difference between 'hold' and 'hinder'. For the moment I will use the word 'suppress', which is used in most modern translations.

What truth then does *the man without the Bible* suppress? Formerly we talked about apostasy in a generation which knew the gospel and turned away from it. The Jews of Jeremiah's day suppressed the truth of the Bible which they had. But what truth does man suppress if he does not have the Bible? We read in verses 19 and 20, 'Because that which may be known of God is manifest in them; for God hath manifested it unto them. For the invisible things of him since the creation of the world are clearly seen, being perceived by the things that are made.'

Paul divides the truth which they suppress into two parts. It is interesting that it is the same two things that Jung says cut across man's will: first of all, the external world; and secondly, those things that well up from inside himself. Jung, though he has no real solution, exactly identifies the two basic things that confront man—man himself, and the external universe. And Paul said long ago, these are the two truths which man, even the man without the Bible, suppresses. As we have seen, Paul preached in other places to the Gentiles without Jews present, in Lystra and on Mars Hill. There too he used exactly the same approach to the man without the Bible.

We should look in more detail at the truth about man

which those without the Bible suppress. The list is fairly long, for man is distinguished from both animals and machines on the basis of his moral motions, his need for love, his fear of non-being and his longings for beauty and for meaning. Only the biblical system has a way of explaining these factors which make man unique.

In Romans 2:15 Paul put special emphasis upon the moral nature of man: 'Which shew the work of the law written in their hearts, their conscience bearing witness, and their thoughts one with another accusing or else excusing.'

God through Paul is saying here exactly what I feel we should say to modern man. Despite what a man may say in theory, he cannot escape being a moral creature. The man who says morals do not exist is not amoral in the sense that he has no moral motions. Men may have different *mores*, but one never finds men without a moral nature.

Take a girl from the streets of London, for example. She may seem absolutely amoral. But if you get her alone and talk to her, you find that she does have her own moral standards. They may be different; they may be very poor. But she is not just a machine. Modern man, as I have said, sees himself in the deterministic situation where morals indeed have no meaning, but he cannot live this way.

We have a startling illustration of this in the Marquis de Sade, who was not only a pornographer, but a real philosopher. Those who are materialists have something to wrestle with in the Marquis de Sade's formulation, something that no determinist has ever been able to answer. The Marquis de Sade says that since everything is chemically determined, then whatever is, is right. Think about that for six months. The simple fact is that, if you are a determinist, there is no way around that conclusion. De Sade is right. And sadism is then the perfectly logical result. Obviously nature made man stronger than the woman: therefore, a man has the right to do anything he wants to a woman. That was de Sade's particular form of sadism. Nobody who holds any concept of determinism, either chemical or psychological, can explain why the Marquis de Sade is wrong. Determinism leads in the direction of cruelty and inhumanity, whether it takes the specific form of de Sade's sadism or not.

But even the Marquis de Sade, who indeed would have claimed that all men were merely determined, could not live this way. If you read carefully from his words and his history, you find that at the end of his life he was in an asylum for the insane, at Charenton. What he was doing hardly seems possible. He was spending his time grumbling about the way he was being treated by the jailors, and he was reading the letters of his wife with meticulous care, having worked out some sort of system whereby he thought he could figure out from the number of letters in the lines the day he was going to get out. Figure it out for yourself. The simple fact is that men, even a Marquis de Sade, may say there is no such thing as morality, and that all is a fixed system, but in their own actions, in their own writing, they demonstrate what they deny.

I have always enjoyed the thought of Krushchev sitting at the United Nations, pounding on the table with his shoe and shouting, 'It's wrong. It's wrong.' Isn't that an interesting thing for a materialist to say? He did not mean that something was merely counter to the best interests of the Soviet Union. He was saying something was wrong.

Moral motions distinguish man from non-man, but so does the need for love. Man feels the necessity of a love that means more than a sexual relationship. Many of the same people who say that love is only sexual go through marriage after marriage, hoping to find something more than physical satisfaction. Even when they say love is only sexual, they are looking for something to make 'love' mean what the heart of man longs to have it mean. They simply cannot live consistently with their own view.

For a few men the need for beauty is the point at which the 'mannishness' of man most clearly shows through, even though on the basis of their own concept of man as a chance configuration of atoms in an impersonal universe, the very meaning of the word 'beauty' is open to question.

All men, however, have a deep longing for significance, a longing for meaning. I was struck just recently by the opening to Will and Ariel Durant's *The Lessons of History*. In the first paragraph they meditate on the cosmic dimensions of the universe, on the fact that the planets will remain not only when individual men are gone but even after the whole race of man is gone. They were impressed with man's transience much as Proust was when he said that the dust of death is on everything human. But as to man's significance all the Durants can point to is a kind of dignity that man has because he can observe the planets and they cannot observe him. It is quite clear: no man—no matter what his philosophy is, no matter what his era or his age—is able to escape the longing to be more than merely a stream of consciousness or a chance configuration of atoms now observing itself by chance.

In an extreme form the longing for significance expresses itself most clearly in the fear of non-being. It has been obvious for centuries that men fear death, but depth psychologists tell us that such a fear, while not found in animals, is for man a basic psychosis: no man, regardless of his theoretical system, is content to look at himself as a finally meaningless machine which can and will be discarded totally and for ever. Even those who seek death and cry for the fulfilment of the death-wish still have a fear of non-being somewhere inside them. I am struck that when you talk to men contemplating suicide, somewhere inside they see themselves as a continuing spectator.

If you go back in art as far as you can go, you find that wherever man is, his essential mannishness is there too. Recently archaeologists unearthed a man that they claim lived something like 30 thousand years ago. They found him buried in a grave of flower petals. Now that's intriguing. You do not find animals burying their dead in flower petals. Or, examine the cave paintings—the largest early work of art which gives us extended content. (I would accept the date of about 20,000 BC for these.) The paintings reveal that those cave dwellers had the same human longings we have. Right there in the midst of the painting are indications that a man is crying out, 'I know within myself that I am more than the dust that surrounds me.' As a matter of fact, there is a theory that explains the cave paintings in southern France and northern Spain as a symbol system speaking out the longings of man. Although it is open to discussion, I think it is probably right, and even if that theory proves not to be correct, still they do show man considering himself as uniquely distinguished from that which is non-man.

We may also mention the testimony of the scholar Levi-Strauss. Though his theories are highly controversial, Levi-Strauss is one of the most important anthropologists in the

87

world today. This French scientist has put forward a notion that has shaken the world of anthropology. No matter where you go, he says, into the past, into the present, to primitive peoples or cultured societies, you find that all men think in the same fashion. Man's thinking has not basically changed along the way. Thus, although primitive tribes may not make high-level, analysed antitheses, there is in tribal thinking a clear antithesis between 'tribe' and 'non-tribe', 'hot' and 'cold', and so forth. The mannishness of man is evident as far back as anybody has been able to penetrate.

Michael Polanyi's arguments concerning the DNA template show much the same thing. Without going into details, let me say simply that Polanyi specifically rejects the chemical determinism of Francis Crick. The chemical and physical properties of the DNA template do not give an explanation of what man is merely on the basis of those chemical and physical properties.

So Levi-Strauss says to look at the thinking of man; wherever you go into the past, into the present, man is man. Polanyi says the DNA template alone does not explain those peculiar things which man is. Mortimer Adler also testifies to the problem of man's uniqueness in *The Difference of Man and the Difference It Makes*. He does not have an answer, but he says there is something different in man and we had better identify it or we will start to treat people as non-human and even more tragedy will result. No matter what his theoretical system is, man knows within himself that he cannot be equated with non-man.

What Paul says in Romans is as up-to-date as the present ticking of the clock—men, even men without the Bible, suppress the truth of what they themselves are. Primitive man, cultured man, ancient man, modern man, Eastern

88

man, Western man: all have a testimony that says that man is more than their own theories explain.

Paul then turns to the second area in which men suppress the truth. In Romans 1:20 he says, 'For the invisible things of him since the creation of the world are clearly seen, being perceived by the things that are made.' So the second testimony man suppresses is the truth of the external world. Jean-Paul Sartre has said that the basic philosophical question of all questions is this: Why is it that *something* is there rather than *nothing*? He is correct. The great mystery to the materialist is that there is anything there at all.

However, it is not only that something chaotic is there but that something *orderly* is there. Einstein understood this very well at the end of his life. According to his friend Oppenheimer and what we know from his own writing, Einstein at the end of his life became a modern mystic. He did not have the answer, he did not return to the Judeo-Christian position or the Bible, but he understood that there had to be a bigger answer because he saw in the universe an order that is indisputable. Einstein worded it beautifully when he said the world is like a well-constructed crossword puzzle; you can suggest any number of words, but only one will fit all the facts. And so Sartre says, 'There's something there,' and Einstein adds, 'Yes. Look at the marvel of its form.' Let us put it another way: there is a distinction between science and science-fiction. In science-fiction you may imagine any kind of universe, but in science you must deal with the universe that is there.

For several years Murray Eden at the Massachusetts Institute of Technology has been using high-speed computers to calculate the possibility of whether on the basis of chance there could be so much complexity in the universe within any acceptable amount of time. His conclusion is that the possibility is zero.

We find the same thing in Charles Darwin himself in his autobiography and his letters. It is amazing that this old man toward the very end of his life keeps saying, 'I cannot believe with my mind that all this was produced by chance.' Not his emotions, but his mind. And he has to excuse the testimony of his intelligence by saying that his mind has just come by evolution from a monkey mind, and who can trust that? But, of course, there is a trick in this. If he could not trust his mind on such a crucial point, how could he trust it to formulate the evolutionary hypothesis itself?

In short, the testimony of the existence and form of the external universe and of man himself, whether in the ancient world or the modern, constantly speaks to man and asks, 'Do your presuppositions—your gods, your philosophy, or your naturalistic science—really explain what is?' Paul is saying that the truth that the man without the Bible suppresses is the truth of *what is*, a truth that surrounds him on every side. The Bible says, 'They are without excuse.' The man without the Bible is *without excuse* because he suppresses the truth of the nature of man and the nature of the external universe.

This is where the different translations of Romans 1:18 referred to above are significant. In the Authorized Version it reads 'hold the truth in unrighteousness' where most modern translations render it as 'hinder' or 'suppress' (*i.e.* 'hold down') the truth in unrighteousness. But 'hold' seems in fact to be the better translation. The explanation, I believe, is as follows. Paul is saying that men—because they refuse to bow to the God who is there and because they hold to their presuppositions as an implicit faith—hold some of the truth about themselves and about the universe, but they do not carry these things to their logical conclusions because they contradict their presuppositions. Therefore, they hold a portion of the truth, but they hold it in unrighteousness. They must hold some of the truth about themselves and the universe for they must live in the universe as God made it, but they refuse to carry these truths to their reasonable conclusions, because, whether they live in the ancient world or in the modern world, they adhere to their false presuppositions. Paul is saying, 'Don't you understand? You really deserve the wrath of God because you, even you without the Bible, hold this testimony in unrighteousness.'

So Paul continues with verses 21 and 22, which we have already examined. Men have become vain in their *reasoning*, their hearts have been darkened and they have become foolishly foolish—holding positions in the very face of what exists. Men then are under God's judgment, not because God has scattered them like a handful of gravel, but because He has treated them as He created them—as significant. Man's own choices have led men where they are. In their own way all men are like the modern young hippie heathen who says, 'Well, I don't care what happens to the next generation, I will take LSD even if it does split the chromosomes. I care only for the moment.' In age after age, men who had the truth have deliberately thrown it away. The world is what it is, not as a result of the cruelty of God to man, but of the cruelty of man to man.

In Romans 1:24 we read, 'Wherefore God also gave them up to uncleanness through the lusts of their own hearts, to dishonour their own bodies between themselves.' Men in our own sociologically and psychologically oriented age have all kinds of explanations for the moral problems of man. But according to the Bible, it is not moral declension that causes doctrinal declension; it is just the opposite. Turning away from the truth—that which is cognitive, that which may be known about God—produces moral declension. The modern artists, the dramatists and the novelists show how far modern man has turned away into moral by-roads. The Bible tells us the cause: men who knew the truth turned away, they are followed by men who do not know the truth, and this results in all sorts of moral turning aside.

Paul repeats this concept three times, in 1:23, 24; 25-27; and from 28 on. He is saying, 'Notice it, and notice it well. You haven't misread. Don't just read it lightly, because I'm going to say it three times so that you'll understand that you read it correctly in the first place. It's because men turn away from God that moral problems arise.'

The message is of special importance for a Christian studying sociology, psychology, ethics or philosophy. It is imperative not to accept minor, secondary causes as to why man sins. Some psychological and sociological conditioning occurs in every man's life and this affects the decisions he makes. But we must resist the modern concept that all sin can be explained merely on the basis of conditioning.

A blatant example of the attempt to explain a man's actions by recourse to conditioning involves Richard Speck, the man who killed eight nurses in Chicago. His psychologist wrote a book saying that Speck could no more keep from killing them than another man could keep from sneezing. This view raises three serious questions. First of all, what about the nurses who were killed, some of them in a very violent fashion? These must then be written off. With this kind of explanation they become zero. Second, what about society? Society and the problems of ordering it also are written off. In such a situation, order in society is merely like a big machine dealing on a machine level with little machines. Third, what about Speck himself? The psychologist's explanation does the most harm to him, for as a man he disappears. He simply becomes a flow of consciousness. He, too, becomes a zero.

In our generation there is a constant tendency to explain sin lightly and think that such an explanation is more humanitarian. But it is not. It decreases the importance and significance of man. Consequently, we can be glad for the sake of man that the Bible's explanation is so emphatic.

Paul repeats it in verse 25: 'They exchanged the truth about God for a lie and worshipped and served the creature [that which has been created] rather than the Creator.' This is the second of the three repetitions.

Paul was thinking of the gods of silver and stone and also the worship of the universe or any part of it. He says men have made such gods rather than worshipping the living God. Even on the basis of what they know themselves to be, they should have known better. Isaiah said 700 years before, 'Aren't you silly to make gods that are less than yourself. You must carry them; they don't carry you. Now isn't it silly to make an integration point that is less than you yourself are.' Paul used precisely the same argument on Mars Hill. Men who refuse to bow before God take the facts concerning the universe and man, push these facts through their own presuppositional grid, fail to carry their thinking to a reasonable conclusion, and so are faced with an overwhelming lie. Idols of stone are obvious lies because they are less than man, but so are non-Christian presuppositions such as the idea of the total uniformity of natural cause and effect in a closed system, the final explanation of the impersonal plus time plus chance, which ultimately makes man only a machine.

So, Paul continues, 'For this cause God gave them up unto vile affections: for their women did change the natural use into that which is against nature: and likewise also the men, leaving the natural use of the woman, burned in their lust one toward another; men with men working that which is unseemly, and receiving in themselves that recompense of their error which was due.'

Usually the first of these sins is taken to refer to lesbianism. But I personally do not think that lesbianism is what is involved. It is parallel to Isaiah 3:16: 'Moreover the Lord saith, Because the daughters of Zion are haughty, and walk with stretched forth necks and wanton eyes, walking and mincing as they go, and making a tinkling with their feet.' That is, Paul is first speaking of heterosexuality which has become twisted. Women turn away from the truth and misuse their natural femininity and all the strong sexuality connected with it. Sexuality here is a neutral word, for the rightness of sex depends on what you do with it. Paul says, the women have used their bodies and their proper sexuality as a man-trap, twisting a good gift of God, which surely Eve had, into that which is wrong. So Paul says, 'You have taken one of the most beautiful things that has ever existed, and ever will exist in the created world, and you have turned it into evil.'

Verse 27 does, of course, refer to homosexuality. As men have turned from the truth they have got their sexuality mixed up. How do we react to homosexuals and lesbians who come to us for help? We must first of all show compassion and not act as though this sin were greater than

94

other sins, or as though we are superior since we are not caught in it. But at the same time we must point out that the practice of homosexuality is wrong. It is not wrong in a way that makes them worse than other sins would do. But its practice is wrong under the absolutes of God.

The third of the three repetitions comes in verse 28: 'And even as they did not like to retain God in their knowledge, God gave them over [or God gave them up] to a mind void of judgment.' The Authorized Version 'a reprobate mind' misses the point. It is a mind void of judgment, a phrase referring back to verses 21 and 22, 'they became vain in their reasoning', religiously but also intellectually foolish. These people do not understand what the universe is, and they do not understand who they themselves are. That sounds very modern indeed.

Paul Gauguin, the French painter, brilliant as he was, provides an excellent example. Following Jean-Jacques Rousseau's idea that man is (or ought to be) autonomous, completely free, he said that what troubled him was that 2 and 2 always equalled 4. He wanted to be so free that on a Tuesday morning at eight o'clock he could say $2 + 2 = 4\frac{1}{2}$.

What Paul is stressing here is that when you turn away from God and follow other presuppositions, the more consistent you are to your presuppositions, the further you get away from reality itself. So you see Gauguin trying to paint an autonomous freedom, a primitive simplicity, and, as it were, stamping his feet and saying, 'If my system is right, somehow or other $2 + 2$ should not always equal 4.'

Let us summarize briefly the course of the argument in this chapter. We began by noticing that Paul speaks in a special way to the man without the Bible, for he has not suppressed the special revelation, that is, the revelation in the Bible, but the general revelation given by the mannish-ness of man and by the external world. It is then plain that the man without the Bible holds the truth in unrighteous-ness, he holds some of the truth about himself and the universe, but he does not follow it to its reasonable con-clusions. Thereafter, a breakdown in morality occurs. God says to man in this position: You are under my judgment. And so the questions arise, how is man without the Bible going to be judged? Is this just?

How is the man without the Bible to be judged by God? Is
God just in His judgment? If you are not merely one of
those who sit under the evangelical umbrella, and if you
have tried to talk to people on the outside, you will know immediately that this is a question that deserves consideration.
Is God really just in judging the man without the Bible?

We read in Romans 1:32 – 2:3, 'Who knowing the
judgment of God, that they which commit such things are
worthy of death [in other words, having a moral nature
regardless of their philosophic system], not only do the same,
but consent with them that do them. Therefore thou art
inexcusable, O man [the man without the Bible], whosoever
thou art that judgest: for wherein thou judgest another,
thou condemnest thyself; for thou that judgest doest the
same things. But we are sure that the judgment of God is
according to truth against them which commit such things.
And thinkest thou this, O man, that judgest them which do
such things, and doest the same, that thou shalt escape the
judgment of God?'

Here is the majority of people scattered all over the world.
Their ancestors (including the last two generations in our
own culture) have turned away from the truth and this
generation is unaware of it. Yet they have had the powerful

testimony of the fact that their own system does not sufficiently explain what is—the mannishness of man and the existence and form of the universe. Further, all men have moral motions, even the modern man who in theory does not believe in morality. Although the standard of moral judgments may be much lower than those set forth in the Bible, moral judgments are still constantly being made.

Let us suppose for a moment that as each baby is born, a tape recorder is placed about its neck. Let us further suppose that this tape recorder works only when moral judgments are being made. Aesthetic judgments, *etc.*, are not recorded, but every moral judgment is. Throughout one's whole life, every real moral motion is recorded upon the tape recorder. Finally, when each person dies and stands before God in judgment, God pushes a button and each person hears with his own ears his own moral judgments as they rolled out over the years: 'You were wrong in doing this. You are wrong in doing that.' Thousands of moral judgments pour forth, and God simply turns and says, 'On the basis of your own words, have *you* kept your own moral standards?' And each man is silent. No person in all the world has kept the moral standards with which he has tried to bind others. Consequently, God says, 'I will judge you upon your own moral statements (those judgments upon which you have bound and condemned others), even if they are lower than moral statements should be. Are you guilty or not guilty?' No-one will be able to raise his voice. The whole world will stand totally condemned before God in utter justice, because they will be judged not upon what they have not known, but upon what they have known and have not kept. So all men must say, 'Indeed I am justly condemned.'

It is most significant that in Romans 2:15, 16, Paul

concludes with this concept in the final two verses where he is addressing the man without the Bible, before he begins to speak to the man with the Bible: 'They shew the work of the law written in their hearts, their conscience bearing witness, and their thoughts one with another accusing or else excusing; in the day when God shall judge the secrets of men by Jesus Christ according to my gospel.'

The Bible emphasizes this in various places. In Matthew 12:36 Jesus says, 'But I say unto you, that every idle word that men shall speak, they shall give account thereof in the day of judgment. For by thy words thou shalt be justified, and by thy words thou shalt be condemned.' There is a theory that all the sounds that have ever been made are still present in the universe, but the wave energy has got so low that no-one can hear them. This may be unlikely, but in some such way we may hear our own words, speaking out as the basis upon which God will judge us. The fact that in hypnosis we may recall a great deal more than we ordinarily can suggests that perhaps deep inside ourselves we never forget anything. God may suddenly use this so that from within ourselves we hear ourselves speak the very words we spoke in our lifetime. Then God will ask, 'Are you condemned or are you not condemned?' And every man in all the world will say, 'It is just, it is just, I am condemned.'

Luke 12:2, 3 reads, 'For there is nothing covered, that shall not be revealed; neither hid, that shall not be known. Therefore whatsoever ye have spoken in darkness shall be heard in the light; and that which ye have spoken in the ear in closets shall be proclaimed upon the housetops.' This is not necessarily just a figure of speech. I believe that men will actually hear their own moral judgments, their own harsh words, being poured out against other men. And they will have to say, 'You are just and I am condemned.'

Revelation 20:12 speaks of the last great judgment: 'And I saw the dead, small and great, stand before God; and the books were opened: and another book was opened, which is the book of life: and the dead were judged out of those things which were written in the books, according to their works.' I have known evangelicals who have been somewhat embarrassed by this, and say that this passage really means that people will be judged on whether they have accepted Christ as Saviour or not. That is not what God says. He says, 'I'm going to judge you by your works, and your works will fail. They will fail on the basis of your own moral judgments against others. No matter who you are or where.' There is no injustice in God's dealings with lost men, because they are judged on the standard by which they have bound others.

You will recall that up to Romans 4 Paul talks about how to become a Christian. From the fifth chapter on he talks to Christians. In Romans 5 there is a titanic statement about the historicity of the space-time fall of Adam. Paul is giving to Christians the explanation of the origin of evil in the area of man. But I think it is highly significant that Paul did not mention this explanation to the man without the Bible. When he talks to the man without the Bible he may say to him, 'I want to ask you a question: do you keep your own moral standards?' I have yet to find the man, who when we are in good empathy, will not say, 'No, sometimes I break them by mistake, but at times I deliberately break them.' And this is what God's Word says will be the basis of the judgment of those who do not have the Bible. The judgment rests upon the individual's true moral choice.

I am perfectly convinced from my experience that short of the biblical position concerning God's judgment of all men you cannot have really good answers for modern man when he asks his questions. Those questions, as I have been emphasizing, are these: Who is man? What is man? Who am I? Does history have any significance? Do I have any significance? And if a Christian is to give answers that are tough-fibred enough to break into the thinking of honest men in the twentieth century, he must have an answer concerning significance that will bear full weight. Moral judgment is made on the basis of the standards a man holds and yet deliberately breaks. Such moral judgment has an effect, not only in this life, but in the life to come. The limitedness of this life never can give significance enough. But here when moral judgment is based on a man's choice which affects his present and future life far down into the reaches of foreverness, suddenly significance breaks like a great bursting bomb. Here is the very opposite of Proust's concept of the dust of death.

The only way that one can get rid of the lostness of men is to give up either one of two things. First is the emphasis upon God's true holiness. This, of course, removes this lostness of men. But the results are disastrous. What is lost is not only God, but man as well. If Nietzsche says, God is dead, Sartre must say, man is dead. For, if you give up the true holiness of God, you give up any moral absolute in the universe, and you are back in a big circle where everything is adrift.

Second, one can give up the significance of history and the significance of man in that history. If neither has significance, then the concept of God's judgment of man can be ignored. But if you do that, man has no meaning. So if you give up the holiness of God, there are no absolutes and morality becomes a zero; if you give up the significance of man, man becomes a zero. If you want a significant man, with absolutes, morality and meaning, then you must have what the Bible insists upon—that God will judge men justly, and they will not be able to raise their voices because of the base upon which He judges them.

This brings me to two conclusions. First of all, in Romans 2:1, Paul moves from abstract statements to personal application: 'Therefore thou art inexcusable, O man.' The third verse repeats the personal emphasis: 'And thinkest thou this, O man?' Paul is not just teaching abstract doctrine. Every doctrine is meant to be practised. Even the doctrine concerning the Trinity is meant to be practised by the way our lives show an understanding of the centrality of personality. And surely Paul's present message is to be practised. All men are going to be judged, and all men are going to be found as those who have totally failed to pass: 'Therefore, O man'—each of us, individually.

Beginning at 2:17 Paul deals with the Jew, the man with the Bible. God says through Paul, 'Just as I have explained that the man without the Bible is to be judged on the basis of the moral standards with which he binds others, I will explain to you, the man with the Bible, that I will judge you upon the higher standards of the Scripture.' And as Paul continues on to 3:9, he concludes: The man with the Bible is no better than the man without the Bible, for both Jews and Gentiles have sinned.

You must understand that God's pass mark is 100 per cent. The reason is that if He is less than perfect or accepts less than perfection, the absolutes are gone! That is what an absolute means; it is a 100 per cent affair. And so God says to the man without the Bible, 'Have you kept 100 per cent the moral judgments with which you bound others?' And to the man with the Bible, 'Have you kept 100 per cent the standards of Scripture?' The answer is no. In Galatians 3:21 Paul writes, 'Is the law then against the promises of God? God forbid: for if there had been a law given which could have given life [or could make alive], verily righteousness should have been by the law.' That is, if God could have given a law so that Jesus did not have to go to the cross, surely He would have done so! He did not send Jesus to the cross as a piece of theatre, as one arbitrary possibility in the midst of other arbitrary possibilities. Rather, since there is no law that man in his rebellion does not break, God consequently had to provide a non-humanist solution for the problem of man.

But in the book of Romans, as early as 1:16, 17, we are confronted with God's unexpected solution: 'For I am not ashamed of the gospel of Christ: for it is the power of God unto salvation to every one that believeth; to the Jew first, and also to the Greek.' Paul says there is a solution for each of us personally—a solution for the universal need of all men. God has provided a solution which fills the practical need *and* can be discussed on Mars Hill without shame. In that solution two great needs are fulfilled: the need for an absolute and the need for the significance of man.

What specifically is this solution? 'For all have sinned, and come short of the glory of God' (3:23). The Greek is stronger: all sinned (aorist tense) in the past, and all are coming short of the glory of God. In the past, we have sinned; in the present, we are sinning. But he continues, 'being justified freely by his grace through the redemption that is in Christ Jesus.' Many Christians have been raised with these words from the Scripture until they have just become god-words. Some may say, 'Oh, I've heard it ten million times, and it grinds through my mind like a gramophone record.'

Smash the record and *listen to the words*! 'Whom God hath set forth [that is, Christ] to be propitiatory through faith in his blood [that is, Christ's finished work in space-time and history, on the basis of the infinite value of His work because of His person as the eternal Son of God], to show his righteousness for the remission of sins that are past, through the forbearance of God.' God has provided a solution whereby His holiness and man's significance can stand and yet not all men will be lost.

Then look at the great 26th verse. People pass by it much too easily, not understanding the wonder of what Paul is saying: 'For the showing at this time his righteousness: that he himself might be just'—that is, that He might keep His holiness, and thus there is an absolute—and yet 'the justifier of him which believeth in Jesus.'

What is being said here? God has provided a way that no philosophy would have thought of. It is a way that would take us by surprise if we were not just thinking by habit. There should be everlasting surprise in it. I stand here. I am significant. God must be holy. Is all lost now that I have sinned? The answer is no! God has provided a propitiation, a substitute. The whole of God's answer rests upon the substitutionary death of Jesus Christ. Because of who He is, His death has infinite value; it can cover every spot; it can remove true moral guilt (and not just the guilt feelings that exist) in the presence of God as the perfect Judge of the universe.

Thus three great things fall into place: God's holiness,

man's significance, and the possibility of man's redemption. It is enough to make one stand up and sing the doxology! Here is an intellectual answer that nothing else has ever presented!

In 2:1-3, Paul brings the message down to the individual: 'Therefore thou art inexcusable, O man.' For Paul's message is not just something for somebody else. It is for every one of us. God *is* holy. There *is* a moral absolute. I *am* significant. I *have* deliberately sinned. I *am* under that wrath of God. Note it well: unless by God's grace I have taken advantage of this unexpected and totally surprising answer to the dilemma, I am under the wrath of God.

Our second conclusion involves our attitude as Christians now that we know that the man without the Bible (not only the bushman but the student and the hippie) is under the judgment of God. It is perfectly true that God in His mercy often brings men into contact with the gospel in very unexpected ways. But we are not to wait like a piece of stone for God to bring men to us. Paul tells us very clearly what our attitude is to be. In 1:14, 15, he says, 'I am debtor both to the Greeks, and to the Barbarians; both to the wise, and to the unwise.' I am a debtor, says Paul, to all classes of men. 'So, as much as in me is, I am ready to preach the gospel to you that are at Rome also.' And although that meant prison and finally death, he was willing to go. He went on in the same way as Jeremiah went on.

Later in 10:13-15, Paul writes, 'For whosoever shall call upon the name of the Lord shall be saved. How then shall they call on him in whom they have not believed? and how shall they believe in him of whom they have not heard? and how shall they hear without a preacher? And how shall they preach, except they be sent? as it is written, How beautiful are the feet of them that preach the gospel of peace, and bring glad tidings of good things!' Paul's response is firm and strong. I am a debtor to be a preacher of the content of the good news. The Christian is called to be the carrier of the content of the good news.

Milton understood properly: Satan was a horrible rebel, but what he did had a large meaning in history. And when men turn and revolt, it has meaning in history. When men who knew the truth turned and revolted against God, it meant that those who followed them in history did not have the content of the gospel. But now there is a gospel. And God turns to those of mankind who know the content, and He says, take the gospel. He continues to honour the way He made man as significant for He now says, I have put the good news into your hands that you might have compassion upon your own kind!

Who are these, regardless of the colour of their skin and the language they speak, scattered over the face of the world? Who are these that do not have the content of the gospel? Who are they? They are *my* kind; they are *my* people; they are not something else. I can really understand them because I am who they are. It is the Christian who knows the real unity of the human race, for we have a common origin; we are of one flesh and blood.

I stand here now, a Christian who has the content of the gospel, and I can say, isn't it wonderful that we have an answer to modern man, who says man is a zero? I can say, you are not a zero. I can say, Proust is wrong. The dust of death is not on everything. There is real meaning that stretches out for ever and ever into the future. Isn't that wonderful? And then if I'm listening and thinking at all, not only to the Word of God, but to the dictates of compassion in my heart, I realize that significance means something more. Significance should make me as the seraphim who cover their faces with their wings. I should put my hands over my face, because now *I am significant*. It is up to me in compassion to take the good news to *my kind*. This is who I now am.

It is Paul again who sounds the warning in 1 Corinthians 9:16: 'For though I preach the gospel, I have nothing to glory of: for necessity is laid upon me; yea, woe is unto me, if I preach not the gospel!' Upon what basis should I preach? Just some nebulous, sociological group pressure from my church or Christian group? Never! Ten thousand times, No! The pressure upon me is this: *I am significant and my kind needs the message that I know.*

Woe to us, woe to our evangelicalism with our lack of compassion. There is a decline in missionary interest across evangelical circles. There is a loss of missionary drive. What is lost? One of two things or both: a real sense of the lostness of the lost or compassion in our hearts. Many of us are intellectually embarrassed to speak of the lostness of the lost. We have been infiltrated by the naturalistic concepts of our own relativistic day. Across evangelicalism there is a great veil; regardless of what men affirm in their statements of faith they no longer are facing the reality of the lostness of their own kind.

And as we have lost the sense of the lostness of the lost, we have also lost compassion. We are hard. Hard! In the newspaper yesterday I saw a picture of a boy and girl in Mexico in the midst of the student riots. They were alive and crying out for help, and two or three minutes later they were dead. What did I think? Did I have any compassion? Or was it just a snapshot in the paper? Just one more picture in a world of things: a girl's face, a boy's face. What do you think when you read of Biafra? What do you think when you see the pictures of those starving people? Do you have any compassion? What I find in evangelicalism is not only weakness in sensing the lostness of the lost, but a tremendous weakness of compassion for the needs of my kind in the present life. Biafra, do you think of it at all? Do you have any interest in helping them—or others in our own country—who need help in this life? And then as a Christian, has your system stood strong and consistent so that as you looked at those starving people in Biafra you also said, 'Yes, they need help in this life; these are my kind, these little children with their sickly light hair. And there's an eternity out there, and these people also need the content of the gospel'? Compassion for the needs of men, that is our need. In the midst of our affluence, compassion for the men in this life and in eternity as we understand the lostness of the lost.

All the church is to be made up of tellers. Not everyone is to be a missionary, not everyone a minister, but there is no Christian that has really become a Christian who does not have laid upon him the admonition of Paul to be a debtor. Everyone is bound to be a teller in his own place, in his own calling, according to the individual vocation which God has given him.

What about missionary giving? Many Christians give their money out of sociological pressure in their group, and that group pressure is often generated by habit. It does not seem to me that most evangelicals give their money out of compassion and a sense of the lostness of the lost of their own kind.

People say to me at times, 'But can you preach the gospel

you have described in the midst of your intellectual presentation? Will twentieth-century man listen? Won't he say it's ugly?' I have never found a man who has thought orthodox Christianity as such is ugly once he understood the titanic answers it gives. What men find ugly is what they see in Christians almost everywhere who hold to the orthodox doctrine that men are lost but show no signs of compassion. This is what is ugly. This is what causes men in our generation to be turned off by evangelicalism. They turn away and say it is ugly and it stinks.

At the conclusion of our study of Jeremiah and his message we said that if there is to be a constructive revolution in the orthodox, evangelical church, then like Jeremiah we must speak of judgment concerning individual men great and small and judgment of the church, the state and the culture which have known the truth of God and have turned away from Him and His propositional revelation. God exists, He is a holy God, and we must know that there will be judgment. And like Jeremiah we must keep on—keep on so speaking regardless of the cost to ourselves. Now having completed our study in Romans we must add this: if there is to be a constructive revolution in the orthodox, evangelical church, we must comprehend and speak of the lostness of the lost, including the man without the Bible. And like Paul we must not be cold in our orthodoxy but deeply compassionate for our own kind.

If we are Christians and do not have upon us the calling to respond to the lostness of the lost and a compassion for those of our kind, our orthodoxy is ugly and it stinks. And it not only stinks in the presence of the hippie, it stinks in the presence of anybody who is an honest man. And more than that: orthodoxy without compassion stinks with God.

In the course of this book we have focused attention on the way God looks at the culture of our day, and at both the men with the Bible and the men without the Bible who have turned away. In this final chapter we will examine the way God looks at those who have the Bible and have responded by believing in the God who is there and are relying on the finished work of Christ in space-time history for the removal of their guilt before a holy God.

As we have seen, Paul says in Romans 1:17 that the just shall live by faith. That is, they shall not only be initially justified by faith, but they shall live existentially by reliance on God and faith in Him. We turn now to see what living by faith means in our twentieth-century world.

First let us note that we who live in the second half of the twentieth century live in an increasingly complicated universe—much more complicated for us than for men just a few years ago. Our telescopes see further and we speak of light years running up into great numbers; the very magnitude of these numbers confuses us. On the other hand, our physicists deal with smaller and smaller particles, and as mass retreats into energy and energy into formulae, reality seems to slip through our fingers. As we look at those light years, we shrink away. And as we look at the tiny particles, we grow like Alice in Wonderland. But our size here does not really help us because we tend to become uncomfortable as we see material reality reduced to sets of mathematical formulae and energy particles dashing about at furious speed. Yet we must understand, if we are going to live as Christians, that while these things indeed are complicated and confusing, nevertheless from the biblical viewpoint the universe is simple.

Let me illustrate this. Imagine a room, the curtains pulled and the doors locked. Let us suppose that this room is the only universe that God has made. Now that would be possible. God could have made such a universe. So let us say that the only universe that exists is this room with the doors locked and the curtains pulled. There is nothing outside at all, absolutely nothing. We are in a universe that can be seen with one look around the room.

Now let us go further. Suppose we have two chairs in this room and that sitting on these two chairs are two men, the only two men in the universe. As we consider them, we find that they differ. One is a totally consistent materialist. As far as he is concerned, the universe is made up of nothing but mass, energy and motion; that is all there is to it. On the other chair sits a Christian who lives in the light of the teaching of the Bible as the propositional revelation of God. And these two sit facing each other in a universe in which they sit alone.

After they have looked at each other for a while, the materialist says, 'Now, I'm going to explore our universe.' And the Christian replies, 'That's fine.' So the materialist begins to analyse the universe, and it takes him a long time. He goes through all the scientific processes that we now use to examine our own universe. He uses the sciences of chemistry, biology, physics, *etc*. He goes back to the periodic table, and behind the periodic table into the atom and examines it. He examines everything from the paint on the wall to the more basic particles. All this takes him a long time.

Finally as an older man, he comes to the Bible-believing Christian and brings him a big set of books, and he says, 'Now here's a set of books, they're nicely bound, and they give in great detail a description of our universe.' So the Christian takes a number of months, even years, to study these books with care. Finally the Christian turns to the materialist and says, 'Well, this is a tremendous work. You have really told me a great deal about my universe that I wouldn't otherwise have known. However, my friend, this is all very fine, but it's drastically incomplete.' And you can imagine this man, who has spent his lifetime pouring out his heart to do his measuring and his weighing, suddenly taken aback. He turns and says to the Christian, 'Well, now, I'm shocked that you tell me it's not all here. What have I missed?' And then the Christian responds something like this: 'I have a book here, the Bible, and it tells me things that you do not know. It tells me the origin of the universe. Your scientific investigation by its very nature cannot do that. And it also says nothing about where you and I as men came from. You have examined us because we, like the paint on the wall, are phenomena in the universe. You've studied something of our psychology and even given me several volumes on it, but you have not told me how we came to be here. In short, you don't know the origin of either the universe or us.

'Furthermore,' the Christian continues, 'I know from this book that there is more to the universe than you have described. There is an unseen portion as well as a seen portion. And there is a cause-and-effect relationship between them. They are not mutually exclusive, but are parts of one reality. It's as if you had taken an orange, sliced it in half, and only concerned yourself with one of the halves. To understand reality in our universe properly, you have to consider both halves—both the seen and the unseen.'

In this sense 'supernatural' is not a good word to describe the unseen portion. We must understand that the unseen portion of the universe is just as natural and as real as is the seen portion. Furthermore, the seen and the unseen are not totally separated. When we do certain things, it makes a difference in the unseen world and things in the unseen world make a difference in the seen world. The Christian would say to the materialist, 'Your volume on the philosophy of history just does not hang together. The reason is that you are only looking at half of what's there: you are only looking at half of history; you do not take into account the unseen portion. Consequently, your philosophy of history will never be sound'. He is right: nobody has ever produced a satisfactory philosophy of history beginning with the materialistic viewpoint. There is too much in the seen world that does not make sense when taken as if it were all there is. One cannot produce a philosophy of history based on only half of history.

Now what happens next? These two men look at each other rather askance because their two primary views of the universe are set one against the other. The materialist replies: 'You're crazy. You're talking about things you can't see.' And the consistent Christian responds, 'Well, you may say I am crazy because I'm talking about things I cannot see, but you are completely unbalanced. You only know half of your own universe.'

Let us notice something extremely important: these two views can never be brought into synthesis. One man is not a little right and the other a little right and a synthesis better than both. These are two mutually exclusive views—one is right and one is wrong. If you say less than this, then you reduce Christianity to a psychological crutch, a glorified aspirin. That does not mean that the Christian cannot glean much detail from the materialist's observation. But as far as the comprehensive view of the universe is concerned, there can be no synthesis. Either this man is right and that man is wrong, or that man is right and this man is wrong. It is a total antithesis.

Pursue their situation further. Suppose that on the wall of their room there is a large clock. All of a sudden it stops. And these two men turn around and say, 'What a pity! The clock has stopped.' The materialist says, 'That will never do, and because there are only you and I in this universe, one of us must clamber up the wall and start the clock. There's nobody else to do it.' The Christian replies, 'Now wait a moment. Yes, it's possible for one of us to climb up and start the clock, but there is another possibility. I may talk to the one who made this universe (one who is not in the universe in the sense of it merely being an extension of his essence) and he can start the clock.'

Here is a tremendous difference in attitude. You can imagine the materialist's reaction. 'Now I know you're crazy. You're talking about someone we can't see starting a material clock.' Anyone who has been doing modern twentieth-century thinking will realize the relevance of this. And I also think we may here see why so many Christians

114

have no reality. They are not certain that it is possible for the God who made the universe to start the clock when a Christian talks to Him.

Let me give you an illustration from experience. Once I was flying at night over the North Atlantic. It was in 1947, and I was coming back from my first visit to Europe. Our plane, one of those old DC4's with two engines on each wing, was within two or three minutes of the middle of the Atlantic. Suddenly two engines on one wing stopped. I had already flown a lot, and so I could feel the engines going wrong. I remember thinking, if I'm going to go down into the ocean, I'd better get my coat. When I did, I said to the hostess, 'There's something wrong with the engines.' She was a bit snappy and said, 'You people always think there's something wrong with the engines.' So I shrugged my shoulders, but I took my coat. I had no sooner sat down, than the lights came on and a very agitated co-pilot came out. 'We're in trouble,' he said. 'Hurry and put on your life jackets.'

So down we went, and we fell and fell, until in the middle of the night with no moon we could actually see the water breaking under us in the darkness. And as we were coming down, I prayed. Interestingly enough, a radio message had gone out, an SOS that was picked up and broadcast immediately all over the United States in a flash news announcement: 'There is a plane falling in the middle of the Atlantic.' My wife heard about this and at once she gathered our three little girls together and they knelt down and began to pray. They were praying in St Louis, Missouri, and I was praying on the plane. And we were going down and down.

Then, while we could see the waves breaking beneath us

and everybody was ready for the crash, suddenly the two motors started, and we went on into Gander. When we got down I found the pilot and asked what happened. 'Well,' he said, 'it's a strange thing, something we can't explain. Only rarely do two motors stop on one wing, but you can make an absolute rule that when they do, they don't start again. We don't understand it.' So I turned to him and I said, 'I can explain it.' He looked at me: 'How?' And I said, 'My Father in heaven started it because I was praying.' That man had the strangest look on his face and he turned away. I'm sure he was the man sitting in the materialist's chair.

But here is the point: there is no distinction between the clock starting and those motors starting. Is it or is it not possible for the God who made the mechanistic portion of the universe to start the clock or start the motors? Is it or isn't it? The materialist must say *no*; the Bible-believing Christian, at least in theory, says *yes*.

We are not dealing with God as though He were a machine. He is personal, and as we pray He does not respond mechanically, but as the Personal-Infinite God. The point is that He is there and He can, and does, act into the universe He has made.

Now then, let us get away from our small universe and suddenly throw wide the curtains, open the doors, push out the walls, the ceiling, and the floor, and have the universe as it is in its full size, as it has been created by God. Instead of two men, there are many men in the universe, but still represented by these two. What we must see is that no matter how deeply we get into the particles of matter or how much we learn by our telescopes and radio telescopes about the vastness of the created universe, in reality the universe is no more complicated than the room we have been talking about. It is only larger. Looking at the bigger universe, we either see it as the materialist sees it or as the Christian sees it: we see it with the one set of presuppositions or the other.

However, what one must realize is that seeing the world as a Christian does not mean just saying, 'I am a Christian. I believe in the supernatural world,' and then stopping. It is possible to be saved through faith in Christ and then spend much of our lives in the materialist's chair. We can say we believe in a supernatural world, and yet live as though there were no supernatural in the universe at all. It is not enough merely to say, 'I believe in a supernatural world.' We must ask, 'Which chair am I sitting in at this given existential moment?' We must live in the present: 'Sufficient unto the day is the evil thereof'—'Give us this day our *daily* bread.' What counts is the chair I am sitting in at any one *existential moment*.

Christianity is not just a mental assent that certain doctrines are true. This is only the beginning. This would be rather like a starving man sitting in front of great heaps of food and saying, 'I believe the food exists; I believe it is real,' and yet never eating it. It is not enough merely to say 'I am a Christian', and then in practice to live as if present contact with the supernatural were something far off and strange. Many Christians I know seem to act as though they come in contact with the supernatural just twice—once when they are justified and become a Christian and once when they die. The rest of the time they act as though they were sitting in the materialist's chair.

The difference between a Christian who is being supernatural in practice and one who says he is a Christian but

117

lives like a materialist can be illustrated by the difference between a storage battery and a light plug. Some Christians seem to think that when they are born again, they become a self-contained unit like a storage battery. From that time on they have to go on their own pep and their own power until they die. But this is wrong. After we are justified, once for all through faith in Christ, we are to live in supernatural communion with the Lord every moment; we are to be like lights plugged into an electric socket.

The Bible makes it plain that our joy and spiritual power depend on a continuing relation to God. If we do not love the Lord as we should, the plug gets pulled out and the spiritual power and the spiritual joy stop. Recall Paul's statement in the benediction, 'The communion of the Holy Spirit be with you all.' In French the word is 'communication'. The reality of the communication of the Holy Spirit who lives within us and who is the agent of the whole Trinity is to be a continuing reality in the Christian's life.

Let us be more specific. The Bible says that Christ rose physically from the dead, that if you had been there that day you would have seen Christ stand up and walk away in a space-time, observable situation of true history. The materialist says, 'No, I don't believe it. Christ is not raised from the dead.' That is unbelief. The new theology is also unbelief because it says either that Jesus was not raised from the dead in history or that maybe He was and maybe He wasn't because who knows what's going to happen in this world in which you can't be sure of anything. The historic resurrection of Christ doesn't really matter, says the new theology; what matters is that the church got a big push from thinking He was raised in history. They see the importance of the resurrection as psychological, even though they say they leave open the door to actual resurrection since we live in a universe that we cannot be very sure of. The old liberalism, the new liberalism and materialism are basically the same. To all of them finally the same word applies: *unbelief*.

But now, here we are, Bible-believing Christians. We stand and say, 'No, I'm not going to accept that. I'm going to speak out against the materialist, and I'm going to speak out against the old and the new liberalism. Christ was raised from the dead, and He did ascend with the same body the disciples saw and touched. Between His resurrection and His ascension He appeared and disappeared many times. He went back and forth between the seen and the unseen world often in those forty days. And then, finally, He took an official departure at the Mount of Olives.' But the Bible says that if Christ is raised from the dead we are supposed to act upon it in our moment-by-moment lives. Its importance is not just in past history.

So the Bible-believing Christian says, 'Well, I believe it!' The materialist says, 'I don't believe it!' and he sits in unbelief. But what shall we say about the man who says, 'I believe it. I believe it', but then does not act upon this in faith in his daily life? I have made up a word for it. I call it *unfaith*.

The Bible tells us plainly that Christ promises to bear His fruit through us. In Romans 7:4 Paul says a very striking thing: 'Wherefore, my brethren, ye also are become dead to the law by the body of Christ; in order that ye should be married to another, even to him who is raised from the dead, in order that we should bring forth fruit unto God.' This verse speaks of each Christian as feminine. At conversion we are married to Christ, who is the bridegroom, and as we put ourselves in His arms, moment by moment, He will produce His fruit through us into the external world. That is beautiful and overwhelming. The bride cannot just stand with the bridegroom at the wedding ceremony. She must give herself to him existentially, regularly, for children to be born to him, through her body, into the external world.

As an example think of Mary and Christ's birth. When Mary heard the annunciation, she did not say to the angel, 'I won't give myself to God in order that the Messiah may be born. What would Joseph think?' It would have been reasonable to say that because we know Joseph was indeed later disturbed. On the other hand, she did not say, 'Now you've told me what is to happen, I can do it on my own.' Mary herself could no more bring forth that baby than any other girl can will a virgin birth. She said the one thing she could say that could be right: 'I am your servant. I give my body into your hands. Do with it as you will.' This was an active passivity. She was passive in that God brought forth the baby. But she was not passive in her will. One can say it this way (and I say it with great care): God would not have raped Mary. She put herself into His hands, and He was the One who produced this marvel of the virgin birth. Of course the virgin birth of Christ to Mary is totally unique, but it can be a profound example to us.

In a very different way the same situation holds with each of us as Christians. Christ wants to bring forth *His* fruit through me into this poor external world. And if I am not acting upon that, I am sitting in the chair of unfaith.

You will notice in Romans 6 (a very sober chapter to the Christian if he reads it with any delicacy of comprehension and feeling) in verses 13, 16 and 19, these words in the present tense: 'Neither yield ye your members as instruments [weapons or tools] of unrighteousness unto sin: but yield yourselves unto God, as those that are alive from the dead, and your members as instruments [weapons or tools] of righteousness unto God.' You continue to be significant after you become a Christian; and either you can yield yourself at any one moment into the hands of Christ for Him to use you as a tool or weapon in this world, or you can yield yourself in that moment as an instrument of unrighteousness even though you are a Christian.

Verse 16 says it again: 'Know ye not, that to whom ye yield yourselves servants to obey, his servants ye are to whom ye obey; whether of sin unto death, or of obedience unto righteousness?' Sitting in the believer's chair, am I yielding myself to Christ for Him to bear fruit through me, or am I yielding myself to be the servant of my old ruler Satan, in which case I am bringing forth death into the external world? The sober thing is that something great is at stake: the whole question of bearing the fruit of the Spirit into the external world, of being an exhibition of the existence of God and His character. The significance of man continues. You are not a programmed computer. Are you going to yield yourself to your bridegroom or are you not? The 19th verse repeats the point: 'I speak after the manner of men because of the infirmity of your flesh: for as ye have yielded your members as servants to uncleanness and to iniquity unto iniquity; even so now yield your members as servants to righteousness unto holiness.'

The unbelieving man says, 'Well, the resurrection—I really don't believe it.' The Christian says, 'I do believe it.' But surely shouldn't we call it unfaith if I am not acting upon it and letting Christ, whom I say is raised from the dead, bring forth His fruit through me?

With this in mind, look at prayer. I feel that the determinism of our own generation has infiltrated us as evangelical Christians so that we do not tend to be praying people. We must understand what prayer is. Prayer, according to the Bible, is speaking to God. The reason why we can speak to God is that He exists, He is personal, and we are made in His image. Since we are made in His image, it should not be surprising that we can be in communication with Him, even though He is infinite and we are finite. When our guilt is removed through the finished work of Christ, communication with God is to be expected. We communicate in a horizontal direction with each other through verbalization. In fact, modern anthropologists say that verbalization more than anything else distinguishes man from non-man. God too communicates to us in verbalization in Scripture, and we communicate to God in verbalization by prayer. It is as simple and as profound as that.

How then does prayer fit into the biblical view of the universe? God made the universe. It is external to Himself, not spatially, but in the sense that it is not an extension of His essence. There is, of course, a machine portion of the universe, but neither God nor man is caught in the machine. There is a uniformity of natural causes, but not in a closed system. The course of nature can be changed—can be reordered—just as when I through a choice of the will interrupt something, for example by reaching over and turning off a light. This act of my will reorders the natural flow of cause and effect. It is in this setting that the Bible sets forth its teaching about prayer.

To return, therefore, to the aircraft: I prayed and God started the aircraft's engines. This is prayer, this is what it is supposed to be. God as well as man can start the motors in the space-time world. Without the true orthodox doctrine of God and man, prayer is just nonsense. You have to understand that there is a personal God and that He has created the universe, which is then not an extension of His essence. If it were, we would have a pantheistic system in which prayer is finally meaningless. At this point there is little difference between the pantheism of the East and many of the New Theologians of the West.

But let us notice that this emphasis must not be just a matter of doctrine. We must really sit in the supernaturalist's chair and pray. If a Christian does not pray, if he does not live in an attitude of prayer, then no matter what he says about his doctrine, no matter how many naughty names he calls the unbelieving materialist, the Christian has moved over and is sitting in the materialist's chair. He is living in unfaith if he is afraid to act upon the supernatural in the present life.

Unfaith turns Christianity into no more than a philosophy. Of course, Christianity is a philosophy—though not a rationalistic one because we have not worked it out beginning from ourselves. Rather, God has told us the answers. In this sense it is the true philosophy, for it gives the right answers to man's philosophic and intellectual questions. However, while it is the true philosophy, our Father in heaven did not mean it to be only theoretical or abstract. He meant it to tell us about Himself—how we can get to heaven, but, equally, how we can live right now in the universe as it is with both the seen and the unseen standing in equal reality. If Christians just use Christianity

123

as a matter of mental assent between conversion and death, if they use it only to answer intellectual questions, it is like using a silver spoon for a screw-driver. I can believe that a silver spoon makes a good screw-driver at certain times. But it is made for something else. It is silly to take the silver spoon that is meant to feed you, moment by moment, and keep it in your tool box to use only as a screw-driver.

But let us look further at the Christian living in unfaith. If the Bible-believing Christian has moved over and is in practice sitting in the materialist's chair, he is living as though the universe were something different from what it is. He is out of step with the universe and is in practice living as though he is more ignorant than a pagan in a jungle.

Suppose three men were sitting together in a jet airliner, one against the window, one against the aisle, and one in the middle. The one at the window is a pagan who hasn't a clue how the airplane flies; he's terrified as the airplane goes up. The man on the aisle knows every nut and bolt in this airplane; he designed it. But he doesn't believe in any supernatural at all. Imagine that you as a Christian are sitting in the middle. Which of these two men on either side of you would best understand the universe? The pagan doesn't have a clue about the airplane, but he knows that there is a seen and an unseen in the universe because he worships demons. The other man knows all about the airplane and he doesn't worship demons, but he also doesn't know that there is an unseen at all. The pagan is less ignorant of reality than the engineer, for the latter is living in only half of the universe. But what about you as the Christian? If you say that the universe has a spiritual dimension and yet do not live like it, you are acting as though you know less than the pagan.

Maybe now we will begin to see why in the evangelical church we often have a feeling of dustiness, unreality and abstraction. I think the reason is that many are functioning as though they knew less about the universe than the pagan knows. They have moved over in unfaith and are living as though the universe is naturalistic. No wonder there is a dustiness! In such a case the evangelical church is a museum of dead artifacts representing what once was a living practice of the doctrine we still say we believe.

If the courses we are giving as teachers are given as though we are sitting in the materialist's chair, is it any wonder that there is unreality? It is possible to teach our subjects that way. We can carry on our church life that way. We can carry on our evangelism that way. And our children then look at us and shake their heads: 'Well, certainly there's something very unreal and mu ty in what I see in my teacher's, my pastor's and my parens' Christian lives.' If we sit in the chair of unfaith, that is the result we should expect.

But let us take note: there are only two chairs, not three. And at this present moment we are either sitting in one or the other. Unfaith is just the Christian sitting in the material-ist's chair. At every moment, existentially, there are before us as Christians the two chairs. After I am a Christian, I do not lose my significance. I am either yielding my life to the living Christ at a given moment or I am not. I am either in one chair or the other.

Which chair are we in? How do we live our lives? What is the set of the way we live? None of us is perfect, this is true. All of us sometimes find ourselves in the materialist's chair. But is this where we habitually sit? Is this how we *usually* teach our subjects? Is this the way we *usually* study? Is it even the way we do what we call 'the Lord's work'? Are we sitting in the chair of unfaith while we are trying to present the doctrines of belief?

Being a Bible-believing Christian, then, not only means believing with our heads, but in this present moment acting through faith on that belief. True spirituality is acting at the given moment upon the doctrines which one as a Christian says he believes.

We must fight the Lord's battles with the Lord's weapons in faith—sitting in the chair of belief. Only then can we have any part in the real battle. If we fight the Lord's battles merely by duplicating the way the world does its work, we are like little boys playing with wooden swords pretending they are in the battle while their big brothers are away at war in some distant and bloody land. The Lord will never honour with power the way of unfaith in His children because it does not give Him the honour. That is true in Christian activities, in missionary work, in evangelism, in anything you name. Living supernaturally does not mean doing less work; nor does it mean less work getting done, but more. Who can do more? We with our own energy and wisdom, or the God who created heaven and earth and who can work in space-time history with a power which none of us has? God exists. And if we through faith stay in the Bible-believing chair moment by moment in practice, and do not move into the chair of unfaith, we and the world will see God act. Christ will bring forth His fruit through us.

As I began this book I brought together the concepts of reformation and revival—the return to pure doctrine and the return of individuals and groups to a proper relationship to the Holy Spirit.

At the conclusion of our study of Jeremiah and his message we said that if there is to be a constructive revolution in the orthodox, evangelical church, then like Jeremiah we must speak of God's judgment of individual men, great and small, and His judgment of the church, the state and the culture, all of which have known the truth of God and have turned away from Him and His propositional revelaion. God exists, He is a holy God, and we must know that there will be judgment. Like Jeremiah we must keep on so speaking regardless of the cost to ourselves. At the conclusion of our study of Romans we added this: if there is to be a constructive revolution in the orthodox, evangelical church, we must comprehend and speak of the lostness of the lost, including the man without the Bible. As with Paul this must not be done with a cold orthodoxy but with deep compassion for our own kind. Finally we must add that these things cannot be done once for all, nor in our own humanistic effort; we must be in the believer's chair moment by moment.

Reformation and revival are related to God's people sitting moment by moment in the believer's chair. And with such reformation-revival will come constructive revolution in the evangelical, orthodox church. Even in the midst of death in the city, the evangelical church can have a really constructive revolution, a revolution that will shake it in all its parts and make it live before God, before the unseen world, and before the observing eyes of our post-Christian world.